A BUDGET FOR

AMERICA'S FUTURE

BUDGET OF THE U.S. GOVERNMENT

FISCAL YEAR 2021

OFFICE OF MANAGEMENT AND BUDGET

THE BUDGET DOCUMENTS

Budget of the United States Government, Fiscal Year 2021 contains the Budget Message of the President, information on the President's priorities, and summary tables.

Analytical Perspectives, Budget of the United States Government, Fiscal Year 2021 contains analyses that are designed to highlight specified subject areas or provide other significant presentations of budget data that place the budget in perspective. This volume includes economic and accounting analyses, information on Federal receipts and collections, analyses of Federal spending, information on Federal borrowing and debt, baseline or current services estimates, and other technical presentations.

Appendix, Budget of the United States Government, Fiscal Year 2021 contains detailed information on the various appropriations and funds that constitute the budget and is designed primarily for the use of the Appropriations Committees. The *Appendix* contains more detailed financial information on individual programs and appropriation accounts than any of the other budget documents. It includes for each agency: the proposed text of appropriations language; budget schedules for each account; legislative proposals; narrative explanations of each budget account; and proposed general provisions applicable to the appropriations of entire agencies or group of agencies. Information is also provided on certain activities whose transactions are not part of the budget totals.

Major Savings and Reforms, Fiscal Year 2021, which accompanies the President's Budget, contains detailed information on major savings and reform proposals. The volume describes both major discretionary program eliminations and reductions and mandatory savings proposals.

GENERAL NOTES

1. All years referenced for budget data are fiscal years unless otherwise noted. All years referenced for economic data are calendar years unless otherwise noted.

2. At the time the Budget was prepared, the United States-Mexico-Canada Agreement Implementation Act (Public Law 116-113) had not yet been signed into law. As a result, the Budget includes a Government-wide allowance to represent the discretionary appropriations included in this proposal, which the Administration transmitted to the Congress on December 13, 2019, the House passed on December 19, 2019, and the Senate passed on January 16, 2020.

3. Detail in this document may not add to the totals due to rounding.

ISBN: 978-1-64143-461-4

Table of Contents

THE BUDGET MESSAGE OF THE PRESIDENT

To the Congress of the United States:

Over the past 3 years, my Administration has worked tirelessly to restore America's economic strength. We have ended the war on American workers and stopped the assault on American industry, launching an economic boom the likes of which we have never seen before.

While our incredible economic turnaround came as a shock to most career politicians in Washington, it is no surprise to millions of hard-working families across the Nation. Their natural talent, ingenuity, and strength simply needed an opportunity to flourish, free from the massive regulations and taxes heaped upon them by their Government.

As my Administration continues to remove these burdens, our economy continues to surpass expectations. We are growing faster than the experts thought possible. The unemployment rate is at 3.5 percent, the lowest it has been in 50 years. And more Americans are working today than at any point in our history.

Today's tremendous job market is leading employers to realize the vast potential of many individuals they previously overlooked. Over the past 3 years, the employment rate of our prime-age workers has skyrocketed, and wages are growing the fastest for historically disadvantaged workers, reversing trends under the previous administration.

With this 2021 Budget, my Administration is placing a special focus on these forgotten Americans, because every individual deserves to experience the dignity that comes through work. The truth is, jobs do not just provide paychecks: they give people purpose; allow them to engage with their communities; and help them reach their true potential. As we have shown, the right policies offer Americans paths to independence rather than trapping them in reliance on Government programs.

The era of putting American workers second and doubling down on the failed policies of the past is over. While job creation during my Presidency has surpassed expectations, the credit belongs to the job creators and workers who risk everything and devote themselves to building a better future for themselves, their families, and their Nation. The Federal Government does not create jobs; hard-working Americans create jobs. My Administration's role is to follow our foundational policy pillars and allow our job creators and workers to do what they do best.

To ensure this economic strength continues, I have called on the Government to reduce wasteful, unnecessary spending, and to fix mismanagement and redundancy across agencies. This includes prioritizing spending for programs that are a core function of the United States Government.

As we enter the 2020's, our Nation confronts new challenges and opportunities. The 21st century requires us to focus on great power rivals; prioritize artificial intelligence, 5G, and industries of the future; and to protect our research and environment from foreign government influence. To meet these challenges and seize these opportunities, we must shift the Government out of its old and outdated ways. This will require each and every Government agency to do more to prepare for the demands of tomorrow.

The following are key priorities of my Administration:

Better Trade Deals. Renegotiated or new trade deals with Canada and Mexico, China, South Korea, and Japan are modernizing international trade and creating freer, fairer, and more reciprocal trade between the United States and our largest economic partners. These deals will enable our country's manufacturing renaissance to continue. Trade deals are in development with the United Kingdom and the European Union, as well as other countries that desire access to the coveted American market. These deals will expand American markets abroad and keep businesses here in America, which means keeping jobs here at home.

Preserving Peace through Strength. To sustain security at home and promote American interests abroad, my Administration has rebuilt the military. A strong military, fully equipped and integrated with our allies and all our instruments of power, enables our Nation to deter war, preserve peace, and, if necessary, defeat aggression against the United States and her people. To that end, my Budget requests $740.5 billion for national defense.

Overcoming the Opioid Crisis. Because of my Administration's aggressive tactics to fight over-prescription of opioids, promote effective treatment for addiction, and secure the border, we are turning the tide of the opioid crisis. Since my term began, we have seen a more than 30 percent decrease in the total amount of opioids prescribed, and deaths from drug overdose fell for the first time in nearly 30 years in 2018.

Failure is not an option when it comes to helping people avoid the pain, suffering, and death caused by addiction. Work must play an integral role in any solution. Research shows that holding a job is a key factor in helping people overcome drug addiction. For the duration of my Presidency, I will continue to promote policies that will beat back this deadly crisis and promote job training and employment opportunities for Americans who are rebuilding their lives after struggling with addiction.

Regulation Relief. Many pundits and Washington insiders laughed when I promised to cut two regulations for every new regulation. They were correct that two-for-one was the wrong goal. Instead, the Federal Government has cut more than seven regulations for every significant new regulation. After only 3 years, my Administration has cut a historic number of regulations, and we have put the brakes on an endless assault of new, costly actions by Federal agencies.

Our commitment to regulatory reform stems from the simple truth that the vast majority of business owners want to do the right thing, comply with the law, and treat their workers fairly. The Federal Government ignored this reality for far too long and abused its authority to go after businesses, especially small businesses and entrepreneurs, in ways that can only be described as arbitrary and abusive.

At the same time, we are maintaining America's world-class standards of environmental protection. Emissions of all criteria pollutants dropped between 2016 and 2018. The United States environmental record is one of the strongest in the world and continues to have some of the cleanest air and water in the world.

American Energy Independence. American energy powers our cities and towns, empowers innovators, drives our economy, and protects our sovereignty. Energy companies across the world are ready to build in our Nation, and permitting reform that cuts red tape shows that we welcome their investments. My Administration continues to support growth in the energy sector by removing unnecessary regulations and unleashing America's vast natural and human resources. Through these actions, the United States is now on track to be a net exporter of crude oil and natural gas for all of 2020, a major milestone not achieved in nearly 70 years. In addition to being the world's largest natural gas producer, we also became the world's top crude oil producer in 2018.

The records of our energy boom are widespread. Energy production has created jobs in areas of the United States where job opportunities were scarce. It also provides enormous benefits to families across the Nation by lowering energy prices. And it further distances us from geopolitical foes who wish to cause us harm. More jobs, lower costs, and American dominance—these are predictable results of our pro-energy policies.

******

Today, there is hope throughout America. There is optimism that was not here before 63 million Americans asked me to work for them and drain the swamp. For decades, Washington elites told us that Americans had no choice but to accept stagnation, decay, and decline.

We proved them wrong. Our economy is strong once more, and America's role as leader of the Free World has been restored.

America is the single greatest country in the world. We must never believe for one moment that this great Nation is destined for a diminished future. When we take hold of our freedom, and take our destiny in our hands, we choose to reject a future of American decline. My 2021 Budget sets the course for a future of continued American dominance and prosperity.

DONALD J. TRUMP

THE WHITE HOUSE,

    FEBRUARY 10, 2020.

BUILDING A BETTER TOMORROW

The Administration's pro-growth policies have ushered in one of the greatest economies in American history. This did not happen by accident. The Trump Economy stands firm on the proven pro-growth pillars of tax cuts, deregulation, energy independence, and better trade deals.

Over the past three years, unemployment rates have dropped to historic lows. The U.S. unemployment rate of 3.5 percent is a half-century low and rates for African Americans, Hispanic Americans, Asian Americans, Americans with disabilities, and Americans without a high school diploma are the lowest on record. Household incomes are rising and wages are no longer stagnant.

Under the previous administration, the recovery was so tepid that the prime-age labor force shrank by roughly 1.5 million. Under this Administration, it has expanded by 2.1 million as previously-forgotten Americans have come off the sidelines. For the first time on record, job openings exceed the number of unemployed workers. The current job market, and the economic confidence this has inspired in consumers, is not a result of past trends during what was the slowest economic expansion since World War II, but the direct result of pro-growth policies put in place over the past three years.

PREPARES FOR A CHANGING LABOR MARKET

While today's great job market is leading employers to realize the vast potential of many individuals who were previously overlooked, the Administration is committed to doing even more to support opportunities for all Americans to experience the dignity and independence work affords. This includes those facing long-term unemployment, lacking necessary job skills, overcoming substance abuse, returning from the justice system, or caught in intergenerational poverty. Reflecting this priority, the Budget creates additional pathways to the jobs of today and the jobs of tomorrow.

Closes the Skills Gap. The Budget doubles the American Competitiveness and Workforce Improvement Act of 1998 fee for the H-1B visa program to provide opportunities to prepare American workers for jobs that are currently being filled from overseas, especially in science, technology, engineering, and mathematics fields.

Increases Vocational Training. The Budget provides resources to assist students too often forgotten—those who would like to pursue good-paying trades without getting a four-year degree. The Budget increases Career and Technical Education by nearly $1 billion to help ensure that every high school has a high-quality vocational program.

Retools the American Workforce for Jobs of the Future. The Administration has provided robust support for apprenticeships to teach students the skills they need to obtain and retain high-wage jobs in a changing market. Since the start of this Administration, nearly 700,000 people have enrolled in apprenticeships.

Combats Drug Abuse and Opioid Epidemic. The Budget invests $5 billion in HHS to combat the opioid epidemic, making critical investments in research, surveillance, prevention, treatment, access to overdose reversal drugs, recovery support services, and research.

This funding includes $1.6 billion for State Opioid Response grants, which supports prevention, treatment, and recovery support services.

Promotes Criminal Justice Reform. At least 95 percent of incarcerated persons will eventually leave prison and return to their community. However, individuals released from State prison have a five-year recidivism rate of 77 percent, and those released from Federal prison have a five-year recidivism rate of 42 percent. The Administration is committed to breaking this cycle by better preparing individuals to reenter communities in meaningful and productive ways.

ENSURES SECURITY TO PROMOTE PROSPERITY

While continuing to strengthen the economy, the Administration also remains committed to strengthening the Nation's physical safety and security to ensure all Americans can prosper. Swift action at the border led to the apprehension and arrest of approximately 5,000 gang members, including nearly a thousand from the infamous MS-13, in 2019 alone, as well as the seizure of millions of pounds of narcotics, including cocaine, heroin, methamphetamines, and fentanyl, which were headed for our community streets and children's schools.

Facing the humanitarian crisis at the border, the Administration has struck new agreements with Mexico, El Salvador, Guatemala, and Honduras to stem the flood of illegal immigration and to protect vulnerable populations from human smuggling networks that profit from their misery. By the end of 2020, the Administration expects approximately 400 miles of new border wall to be completed on the southern border; an additional 600 miles of new border wall will be completed in the coming years with funding made available from 2017 to 2020. In the meantime, the Administration has released a plan for updating immigration and asylum laws to encourage legal migration, promote application based on merit, and support refugees in need of protection from persecution.

The Budget provides funding sufficient to hire an additional 4,636 Immigration and Customs Enforcement staff including: law enforcement officers; immigration court prosecuting attorneys; and critical support staff, to reach a total of 6,000 staff to carry out this vital security mission. In addition, the Budget includes $1.6 billion to continue the important work of modernizing the U.S. Coast Guard vessels and aircraft that patrol the Nation's coastal borders.

Abroad, the Budget promotes an America First agenda by advancing the four pillars of national power—economic competitiveness, national security strength, fair and free trade, and foreign partnerships that match action and resources with intent and rhetoric. The Administration has rebuilt our great and powerful military to deter aggression, counter adversaries, and fight and win wars. Through bold action, the Administration has lead and won efforts to rebalance our trade relationships, fight theft of American intellectual property, open markets to American goods, and bring jobs home to hardworking Americans.

STOPS AN UNSUSTAINABLE TRAJECTORY

Unsustainable Federal deficits and debt are a serious threat to America's prosperity. Gross Federal debt is now more than $23 trillion. The 2019 deficit was $985 billion—the largest since the Great Recession—and will climb above $1 trillion this year and for years after.

Such high and rising debt will have serious negative consequences for the budget and the Nation. It slows economic growth, as the costs of financing the debt crowds out more productive investments and could eventually limit the Federal Government's ability to respond to urgent national security needs, invest in key priorities such as infrastructure, and enact other pro-growth policies. In fact, by 2021, the United States will be spending more money on paying for the debt than for the budgets of the Departments of Veterans Affairs, Justice, Homeland Security, and the National Aeronautics and Space Administration combined.

Federal borrowing also competes for funds in the Nation's capital markets, threatening higher interest rates, and crowding out new investment by the private sector that could create jobs and raise wages.

If America's spending and debt crisis are not addressed and lower economic growth continues, American families will see a much lower standard of living. Higher interest rates would make it harder for families to buy homes, finance car payments, or pay for college. Fewer education and training opportunities stemming from lower investment would leave workers without the skills to keep up with the demands of a more technology-based, global economy. In addition, continued growth of debt and deficits will constrain American families' ability to improve their lives and the lives of their children by claiming a larger share of family income for taxes. It is the children and grandchildren of today's taxpayers who will bear the burden for this recklessness.

The President has laid out a vision to drive down deficits and debt through spending restraint in every Budget he has submitted to the Congress. This Administration's Budgets have proposed more spending reductions than any other Administration in history. This year's Budget includes $4.4 trillion in savings—bringing deficits down each year, and putting the Federal Government on a path to a balanced budget in 15 years. This spending restraint includes targeted reductions and eliminations of low-value programs, and a number of policies to improve payment accuracy and eliminate wasteful spending in mandatory programs. The Budget also reflects restraint in non-defense discretionary (NDD) spending, which the Budget proposes to keep five percent below 2020 NDD spending levels, and reduce spending in future years. Such

spending restraint, coupled with the President's tax cuts and deregulatory policies, will keep the U.S. economy thriving and America prosperous for generations to come.

Unfortunately, the Congress continues to reject any efforts to restrain spending. Instead, they have greatly contributed to the continued ballooning of Federal debt and deficits, putting the Nation's fiscal future at risk.

The Administration cannot simply sit by while the Congress continues to spend. In addition to providing a clear road map to a more fiscally responsible future in the Budget, the Administration is using all available tools and levers to restrain spending. This includes reinvigorating Administrative pay-as-you-go, otherwise known as Administrative PAYGO—which imposes a budget-neutrality requirement for discretionary agency actions—to ensure that Executive Branch agencies are also fiscally responsible, as well as the revitalization of tools such as rescissions. The Budget also includes a number of regulatory actions that can be achieved with current authorities to improve program efficiency and eliminate wasteful spending.

Implementing the real spending restraint proposed in the 2021 Budget, coupled with other pro-growth policies, will keep the economy thriving and America prosperous for generations to come. America can choose a new path that the Administration offers with the Budget, or continue the path the Congress and Washington have followed, which will ensure future generations are saddled with less prosperity, less financial control over their lives, and less freedom.

COUNTERING EMERGING THREATS

As the United States enters the 2020s, the threats America faces as a Nation are rapidly shifting and evolving. While the American people still face dangers posed by Islamist terrorists and transnational criminals, America also faces challenges by resurgent rival nation-states, including China and Russia. The Budget reflects the need for a new American posture to match the realities faced in this new era.

To sustain American security at home and promote U.S. interests abroad, the Administration has rebuilt the military, invested in the well-being of America's servicemembers, expanded U.S. capabilities to fight in emerging theaters, and refocused U.S. defense priorities on contemporary threats.

It is not just U.S. troops and Government agents on the front lines anymore. It is U.S. businesses, universities, and social groups. A rural hospital, family-owned business, or private citizen is no match against a nation-state such as China, Iran, North Korea, or Russia attempting to hack their network. Threats to U.S. security are coming in an ever-increasing variety of forms against an ever-expanding variety of targets.

More than ever, each adversary has the ability to use modern technology to harm U.S. economic prosperity, limit freedom around the globe, and undermine America's superior military advantage. Attacks on America's devices and networks, which are critical to U.S. economic well-being and security, are omnipresent. With an estimated 75 billion devices connected to the internet by 2025, it is clear these vulnerabilities will only increase. It is all too easy for a rogue nation-state or cyber-criminal to target a weak link in a global supply chain that relies on the internet in order to cripple America's economy or infrastructure—with little fear of attribution or reciprocity.

To stay ahead of these threats, the U.S. Government must shift out of the old, staid ways in which it has historically operated, and focus more on the challenges posed by great power rivals and emerging technology. Instead, a whole-of-Government approach to overcome these rising risks by preparing to meet the demands of tomorrow is needed. Such an approach includes prioritizing artificial intelligence (AI), 5G, and other industries of the future.

The 2021 Budget reflects the need to reposition American economic, military, and diplomatic postures to ensure that everything America holds dear—individual liberty, the rule of law, a democratic system of government, and opportunity for all—is protected. Preserving American leadership and values requires an America First agenda that must be promoted by advancing four pillars of national power—economic competitiveness, national security strength, free and fair trade, and foreign partnerships that match action and resources with intent and rhetoric.

We have rebuilt America's great and powerful military to deter aggression, win wars, and inflict punishment on U.S. adversaries to defend America and her people, values, and friends at home and abroad. Through significant investments in emerging warfighting domains such as space through the creation of the United States Space Force, and advancement of modern technologies, including reinvigorating missile defense, hypersonics, cyber, and AI, this Administration will put America in the driver's seat when negotiating with America's adversaries from a position of strength.

PROTECTING AMERICA'S ECONOMY

Protecting America's vital economic interests against those who would do America harm has never been more important. Great power rivals, such as China, have engaged in cyber-enabled economic warfare against the United States and its allies. These adversaries target key components of America's economy. They seek to gain an advantage against the United States by stealing U.S. intellectual property and personal data, as well as interfering with America's critical infrastructure. These actions threaten the foundations of the American way of life.

The Budget focuses on overcoming the many challenges posed by great power rivals that target U.S. economic stability.

Better Trade Deals. For decades, unfair trade practices have weakened the U.S. economy and exported U.S. jobs overseas. The Administration is advancing fair and reciprocal trade through agreements with Mexico, Canada, South Korea, and Japan, and through ongoing negotiations with the United Kingdom, China, and European countries. These agreements open new markets for American exports and create jobs while protecting American intellectual property and America's domestic producers.

Industries of the Future. The Budget prioritizes accelerating AI solutions. Along with quantum information sciences, advanced manufacturing, biotechnology, and 5G research and development (R&D), these technologies will be at the forefront of shaping future economies. The Budget proposes large increases for key industries, including doubling AI and quantum information sciences R&D by 2022 as part of an all-of-Government approach to ensure the United States leads the world in these areas well into the future.

Energy Independence. The Budget recognizes and supports the emergence of the United States as a top producer of energy in the world, becoming a net exporter of petroleum in late 2019 and projected to be one for the 2020 calendar year—a position of energy independence the United States hasn't been in since the 1940s.

Defending Government Networks and Critical Infrastructure. The Department of Homeland Security (DHS) continues to play a major role in securing and building cybersecurity resilience for the Nation's most critical infrastructure, including Government networks. DHS, in partnership with key stakeholders, identifies and manages the most critical national cybersecurity risks. The Budget includes more than $1.1 billion for DHS's cybersecurity efforts.

Addresses the Federal Cybersecurity Workforce Shortage. To face today's threats and prepare for tomorrow's, America must have a workforce that is trained and skilled in cybersecurity. Today, there are simply not enough cyber professionals in Government service. The *Delivering Government Solutions in the 21st Century* plan and Executive Order 13870, "America's Cybersecurity Workforce" included several initiatives to solve the Federal cybersecurity workforce shortage, establishing unified cyber workforce capabilities across the civilian enterprise. The Budget includes funding to support DHS's Cyber Talent Management System and for the Cybersecurity and Infrastructure Security Agency, which would lead a Government-wide cybersecurity workforce program for all Federal cyber professionals.

REBUILDING AMERICA'S MILITARY

Sharpens America's Advantage in an Increasingly Competitive Strategic Landscape. The Budget prioritizes funding for programs that would deliver warfighting advantages against China and Russia and sustains efforts over the last three years to focus defense investments in modernization, lethality, and innovation that provide the Nation's troops a competitive advantage over all adversaries.

Modernizes Key Capabilities to Build a More Lethal Joint Force. The Budget prioritizes investments in U.S. air, sea, land, space, and cyber capabilities that would support operations to ensure military superiority. Critical investments include procuring next generation fighter aircraft and new battle force ships, modernizing Army armored brigade combat teams, and fully funding recapitalization of the strategic ballistic missile submarine fleet. The Budget also assesses modifications to existing missile defense capabilities to defend the U.S. homeland, providing additional coverage on a faster timeline.

Grows and Reorganizes the U.S. Military to Better Compete in Emerging Domains. The Budget supports the growth of the recently established United States Space Force, the sixth branch of the U.S. Armed Forces, to ensure that the United States can protect and defend America's national interests in space.

Invests in the Nation's Men and Women in Uniform. The Administration understands that America's security and freedom is ensured by the sacrifices of the men and women who wear the uniform and is investing in their well-being and that of their families. On the heels of growing annual pay raises for America's troops throughout this Administration, the pay raise effective January 1, 2020, was the first over three percent in a decade. The Budget proposes an additional raise in the coming year.

Secures the Capability to Supply Vital Military Resources in the Long Term. The Administration has directed the first whole-of-Government assessment of U.S. manufacturing and defense supply chains since the 1950s.

ENGAGING AMERICA'S ALLIES TO ADVANCE FREEDOM

Realigns Burden-Sharing to Encourage Greater Engagement from Allies. The Budget recalibrates American contributions to international organizations to a more sustainable level, engaging U.S. allies to similarly invest in peace and stability. The United States will continue to press its allies to give more in providing for their own defense; frequent increases in North Atlantic Treaty Organization (NATO) ally funding has been a result. Further, the United States will continue to emphasize and enforce a road to self-reliance in foreign assistance to ensure that there is a positive return on investment for each American taxpayer dollar.

Expands Defense Financing for America's Allies. The Budget proposes Foreign Military Financing (FMF) loan and loan guarantee programs for NATO and major non-NATO allies to complement traditional FMF grant assistance. These tools would bolster security, improve battlefield interoperability, and support American domestic economic interests, and would increase opportunities for allies and partners to build their militaries around U.S. innovation and quality, while transitioning away from inferior equipment from foreign adversaries.

Frustrates Chinese Efforts to Shape the Indo-Pacific in Its Image. The future of the Indo-Pacific, which contains roughly half the world's population and many of the fastest growing economies, is critical to U.S. security and long-term economic interests. The Budget reflects a strong Administration commitment to ensuring that the region remains free, open, and independent of malign Chinese influence with funding that supports democracy programs, strengthens security cooperation, improves economic governance, and facilitates private sector-led economic growth. The Budget also provides $30 million for the Global Engagement Center to counter Chinese propaganda and disinformation.

STOPPING WASTEFUL AND UNNECESSARY SPENDING

The President's pro-growth policies have set in motion one of the strongest economies in American history. The Budget ensures that the U.S. economy can remain resilient and that the United States maintains its global leadership by prioritizing funding for the most vital functions of Government. However, a bloated Federal Government, with duplicative programs and wasteful spending, remains a critical threat to America's future.

Each year, billions of taxpayer dollars are wasted on programs that are duplicative, unnecessary, and ostensibly without priority. This has reduced the ability of the Federal Government to meet its constitutional responsibilities to the American people.

As with the Administration's past Budgets, the 2021 Budget continues to propose strategic reductions in spending. In fact, the Administration's Budgets have put forward more spending reductions than any other in history. This effort is the foundation of a commitment to the American people to restore trust in their Government.

While the Administration has prioritized the core responsibility of national security by rebuilding its great military, securing America's borders, and advancing emerging technologies, continued waste across the Government must be addressed. The Budget looks to reduce wasteful and unnecessary spending, and put in place procedures to keep a vigilant eye on fraud, abuse, and negligence with taxpayer dollars.

RESIZING THE BUREAUCRACY TO FIT THE CONSTITUTION

The Federal Government was envisioned by the Founders to be one of limited powers, protecting the unalienable rights of individuals. However, over the past century, the size and scope of the Federal Government has overrun these constitutional guardrails. Today, there are more than two million Federal civilian employees with millions more who are paid entirely by Government contracts and grants.

Taxpayers have repeatedly watched the Federal Government respond to any problem with the creation of new agencies, new programs, and new spending initiatives, instead of reorganizing, or repurposing what is already available within the vast bureaucracy. As a result, there are hundreds of programs in the Federal Government that have outlived their mission, duplicate efforts, or operate below peak efficiencies because of fragmented responsibilities between agencies. This wasteful spending has been a contributing factor to the Government's deteriorating fiscal health as reflected in the *Financial Report of the United States Government*.

The Administration believes the American people deserve better from their Government.

DEFINING THE PROBLEM

There are universal tenets on which broad bipartisan action to reduce spending should be based:

First, all Government programs should have a direct, clear, and immediate purpose and not duplicate other programs.

Second, all Federal spending should provide a necessary public service and serve a clear national interest. American taxpayers deserve a Government that is not spending taxpayer dollars to support a Muppet Retrospectacle in New Zealand or millions to prepare religions for discovering extraterrestrial life (which are real, and unfortunate, examples of wasteful spending).

Third, all spending should fund its intended purpose and reach its intended recipient. That is, there should not be improper payments that result in monetary loss to the Government, such as when beneficiaries receive an incorrect amount, or deceased individuals continue to receive assistance.

Fourth, the Government should be frugal and strive to avoid overpaying for items.

Fifth, the Federal Government should spend only the amount necessary to achieve intended goals, and all expenditures should be assessed on that basis.

Sixth, each dollar spent should be measured by its effect on actual outcomes.

CATEGORIES OF WASTE REQUIRING ACTION

Using these guidelines, the Budget attempts to begin restraining and refocusing taxpayer resources in the following five ways:

- Eliminating Duplicative Programs;

- Eliminating Programs with No Proper Federal Role;

- Putting an End to Improper Payments;

- Conducting Oversight of Spending Categories; and

- Stopping Improper End-of-Year Spending.

The Budget's *Major Savings and Reforms* volume describes the major savings and reform proposals included in the Budget. In total, the discretionary proposals highlighted in the volume

would save $48 billion in 2021.

ELIMINATING DUPLICATIVE PROGRAMS

In May 2019, the U.S. Government Accountability Office released its ninth annual report with recommendations to reduce overlap, duplication, and fragmentation in Federal programs. This annual report identifies opportunities for cost savings, and a better customer experience for the American people, through three types of common inefficiencies in Government:

Fragmentation: when more than one Federal agency, or more than one component within an agency, is involved in the same broad area of national need and there are opportunities for improving service delivery.

Overlap: when multiple agencies or programs have similar goals, engage in similar activities or strategies, or target similar beneficiaries.

Duplication: when two or more agencies are engaged in the same activities or provide the same services to the same beneficiaries.

The Budget addresses many of these inefficiencies by reforming, reducing funding for, and in some cases eliminating these programs. Examples include:

- **U.S. Department of Agriculture (USDA) Programs that Provide Assistance to the Private Sector, Do Not Require Matching Funds, and Duplicate Other Federal Assistance.** For example, USDA has the authority to make crop loss payments under both a disaster assistance program and the crop insurance program, masking market forces and allowing some farmers to receive payments in excess of 100 percent of their loss.

- **Overlapping Elementary and Secondary Programs.** The Budget proposes to consolidate 29 overlapping elementary and secondary programs into a new block grant to States and school districts. This consolidation would allow those closest to students to meet the needs of their students and families. While increasing flexibility, the new block grant also saves taxpayers $4.7 billion.

- **Disjointed Workforce Programs.** The Federal Government spends $19 billion per year on more than 40 workforce development programs across 15 agencies. The Budget begins the work of rationalizing this convoluted system by eliminating ineffective, unproven, or redundant job training programs.

- **Duplicative Health Professional Training.** The Budget eliminates funding for 14 health professions training programs in the Department of Health and Human Services. There are 91 Federal programs that support the training of healthcare professionals, across the Departments of Defense, Education, Health and Human Services, and Veterans Affairs.

- **Readily Available English Learning Materials.** Several U.S. institutes of higher learning offer free or low-fee English learning materials online. The Budget proposes to eliminate nearly $2 million for duplicative Government-funded online English-language learning programs and materials for foreign audiences. The U.S. Agency for Global Media spends $1.5 million on Voice of America's English Learning programming, which produces relatively low-quality educational videos. Similarly, the State Department creates and runs Massive Open Online Courses for English learning.

There are also Federal programs that duplicate the efforts and expenditures of State and local governments or the private sector. For example, the Budget proposes to eliminate:

- **The Department of Commerce's Economic Development Administration Grant Programs.** The programs are duplicative of other economic development programs within the Federal Government, as well as State and local efforts.

- **Power Marketing Administration Electricity Transmission Assets.** The vast majority of the Nation's electricity needs are met through for-profit investor owned utilities. Increasing the private sector's role encourages a more efficient allocation of economic

resources and mitigates unnecessary risk to taxpayers.

- **The Federal Emergency Management Agency's (FEMA) Continuing Training Grants.** The grants, which support partners to develop and deliver training to prepare for disasters, among other grant programs, are proposed for elimination because they are duplicative of other Federal grant programs or other State or local programs, and are primarily the responsibilities of States and localities.

- **USDA Rural Business Service Programs.** These programs have spent over a billion dollars during the last 10 years supporting already successful businesses that could qualify for private sector capital. For example, the Value-Added Producer Grant program has provided over $3 million to wineries and vineyards in 2018, including grant funding to promote wine slushies.

- **The Department of Housing and Urban Development's (HUD) HOME Investment Partnerships Program.** The Budget eliminates the HOME program, recognizing a greater role for State and local governments and the private sector in addressing affordable housing needs.

ELIMINATING PROGRAMS WITH NO PROPER FEDERAL ROLE

There are also programs where the Federal Government's role is unclear and unnecessary. For example:

- **Applied Energy Programs.** Private sector-led research and development (R&D) tends to focus on near-term cost and performance improvements where the certainty of profit generation or successful market entry are greatest. The Federal role in energy R&D is strongest at the earlier stages, where the greatest motivation is the generation of new knowledge and the proving of novel scientific or technical concepts. While progress has been made over the past three years, the Budget continues to refocus these programs on earlier-stage R&D energy challenges.

- **Education and Research Centers (ERCs) within the National Institute for Occupational Safety and Health.** The ERCs were created in the 1970s to develop occupational health and safety training programs in academic institutions. Almost 50 years later, the majority of public health schools include this coursework, and many academic institutions have developed specializations in these areas. The Budget would stop directing Federal funding to support academic salaries, stipends, and tuition and fee reimbursements for occupational health professionals at universities.

- **Department of the Interior (DOI) Highlands Conservation Act Grants.** The Budget eliminates grant funding ($20 million in 2019) under the Highlands Conservation Act for non-Federal land acquisition projects in highland States. These grants serve no clear Federal purpose and divert limited DOI funding from managing national parks, refuges, and public lands.

- **Funding for the National Park Service's Save America's Treasures Grants.** The grants are used to support preservation of non-Federal historic buildings, arts, and published works.

- **The National Endowment for the Arts (NEA)/National Endowment for the Humanities (NEH).** Activities funded by NEA/NEH are not considered core Federal responsibilities, and make up only a small fraction of the billions spent each year by arts and humanities nonprofit organizations.

- **The Corporation for National and Community Service (CNCS) (including AmeriCorps).** Funding paid volunteerism and subsidizing the operation of nonprofit organizations is outside the proper role of the Federal Government. To the extent these activities have value, they should be supported by the nonprofit and private sectors and not with Federal subsidies provided through the complex Federal grant structure run by CNCS.

PUTTING AN END TO IMPROPER PAYMENTS

Every year, the Federal Government makes improper payments. This is an obvious form of wasteful spending, and it costs taxpayers over $70 billion per year. While the Government has spent years working to eliminate this issue, more must be done to increase appropriate and careful stewardship of taxpayer funds.

Prior to this Administration, the Federal Government failed to properly prioritize its efforts regarding eliminating improper payments. For instance, Agencies spent more time complying with low-value compliance activities than researching the underlying causes of improper payments and building the capacity to help prevent future improper payments. Although working to reduce all improper payments is an important goal, the Administration has prioritized efforts to end the most egregious abuses, such as improper benefits sent to deceased persons that cost taxpayers over $800 million per year.

The Getting Payments Right Cross-Agency Priority Goal is a key part of the President's Management Agenda. This agenda is focused on new strategies to reduce monetary loss because protecting taxpayer money and making sure it is serving its intended purpose is a fundamental responsibility of the Federal Government. Progress toward this goal has paved the road for improved prevention of improper payments by: improving the transparency of payment integrity data on *https://paymentaccuracy.gov*; identifying 160 new data sets currently being used by Federal programs for pre-check of payment eligibility; identifying root causes of monetary losses across 57 programs; and identifying eight mitigation strategies with potential for broad impact across multiple programs.

The Budget provides many opportunities for the Congress to achieve maximum savings to the Government, while also considering and balancing costs, risks, and program performance. Families and small businesses could not afford to operate in the careless way that the Federal Government has been operating. CEOs at large companies have lost their jobs for similar carelessness, and rightfully so. The Administration believes that Government can do better with American's hard-earned tax dollars.

CONDUCTING OVERSIGHT OF SPENDING CATEGORIES

The Administration has begun identifying spending categories that often become a catchall for wasteful spending. These include:

- Travel;
- Workshops and Conferences;
- Subscriptions;
- Receptions and Refreshments;
- Marketing; and
- Entertainment.

Not every expenditure within these categories is wasteful, but experience has demonstrated that additional scrutiny is necessary. If an agency wants to spend taxpayer dollars on motivational speakers or grants to already successful businesses, it should be prepared to substantiate its request and verify that it is the best and most efficient use of money.

Of the $550 billion spent annually through Federal acquisition, over $350 billion is for common goods and services such as software, cellphones, and information technology. Federal agencies have traditionally purchased goods and services in a fragmented manner, depriving taxpayers of the benefits of the U.S. Government's position as the largest buyer in the world. Category management is a commercial best practice for buying common goods and services that has been adopted by the Administration. Organizing common purchases using category management principles provides agencies with the data and tools they need to comparison shop, obtain volume discounts, and negotiate better deals so taxpayer dollars can be spent on caring for veterans and families.

Applying such leading category management practices has allowed the Government to save taxpayers over $27 billion since 2017 and eliminate 31,000 duplicate contracts, all while the Administration continues to exceed annual small business contracting goals.

STOPPING IMPROPER END-OF-YEAR SPENDING

September, the end of the Federal fiscal year, is traditionally characterized by a surge in spending. Studies of Federal spending have shown that one out of every nine dollars in Federal contracts was spent in the last week of the fiscal year. On average, the Federal Government spends $3.2 billion a day in contracts. In the last two days of 2018 alone[1], agencies spent $10 billion a day.

According to data from the nonprofit group, Open the Books, of the $97 billion spent by 67 Federal agencies in a "Use It or Lose It" spending spree in the final two days of 2018, expenditures included:

- china tableware ($53,004);
- alcohol ($308,994);
- golf carts ($673,471);
- musical equipment, including pianos, tubas, and trombones ($1.7 million);
- lobster tails and crab ($4.6 million); and
- workout and recreation equipment ($9.8 million).

While there are many reasons that last-minute improper spending occurs, there are currently misaligned incentives in the budgeting process which encourages this practice. Agencies recognize that if significant balances are left in their accounts at the end of a fiscal year, the Congress will likely reduce their topline budget in future fiscal years.

While some end of year spending is legitimate, the Administration is committed to closely scrutinizing how it spends money at the end of the fiscal year, and curtailing wasteful and questionable purchases. Americans deserve a Government that is meticulous at avoiding wasteful and unnecessary spending.

[1] https://www.openthebooks.com/the-federal-governments-use-it-or-lose-it-spending-spree--open-the-books-oversight-report/

HISTORIC RED TAPE RELIEF

Since taking office, the President has reinvigorated the economy through a historic regulatory reform agenda. The President's regulatory agenda is enabling American workers and businesses to drive the economy to record-breaking heights. The American people can feel the effects of economic freedom as the Administration eliminates unduly burdensome regulations and pulls back the long reach of Federal mandates.

In 2019, the Administration issued more than four deregulatory actions for every one new significant regulation and saved the American people $13 billion in overall regulatory costs. After three years in office, the deregulatory-to-regulatory action ratio has been a remarkable 7.4-to-1, resulting in a total of $51 billion in net regulatory cost savings for the American people. This is a stark contrast to the $420 billion in net regulatory costs imposed by the Obama Administration during the same amount of time. The President's regulatory reform agenda represents a fundamental change of direction for the Federal Government. The strategy is simple: by eliminating or amending costs that are duplicative, unnecessary, ineffective, or unduly burdensome, the Administration is unleashing the ingenuity, determination, and know-how of the private sector, which has always been the principal driver of American prosperity.

Comprehensive regulatory reform has provided relief to millions of Americans. Small businesses are the job creators that drive economic growth. The Administration's regulatory reform agenda so far has been a great one for the American small business owner. Over the past year the Administration has:

- Cleared the way for small businesses to help their employees save, by making innovative retirement plans available for small businesses to use;

- Freed American farmers and builders to use their land as they see fit, not as Washington demands; and

- Stopped the war on energy production and brought American families cheaper, more reliable power.

In addition, the Department of Health and Human Services removed multiple healthcare burdens, saving over $600 million in regulatory costs.

The Administration plans even bolder efforts during the remainder of 2020. Agencies plan deregulatory actions on Federal fleet mandates for the Corporate Average Fuel Economy standards, Waters of the United States, and automated vehicles, resulting in even more benefits for the American people. While continuing to protect health and safety, the President's regulatory reform allows individuals and small businesses to produce and innovate. These bold actions will support job creation, spur innovation, and yield billions of dollars in benefits for American businesses and families.

However, deregulation is not only about dollars and cents. That is why the President signed two important Executive Orders in 2019 to stop Government bullying of small businesses and families: Executive Order 13891, "Promoting the Rule of Law Through Improved Agency Guidance Documents;" and Executive Order 13892, "Promoting the Rule of Law

Through Transparency and Fairness in Civil Administrative Enforcement and Adjudication." These Executive Orders protect Americans against secret or unlawful bureaucratic interpretations of rules and put in place safeguards against unfair or unexpected penalties.

Getting Washington out of the way promotes the American dream. The Administration's commonsense regulatory policy has renewed confidence in the economy so the American people can once again confidently invest in their families, businesses, and future. American families and entrepreneurs are not the enemy, and it is long past time the Federal Government stopped treating them as such.

DELIVERING A MORE RESPONSIVE, AGILE, AND EFFICIENT GOVERNMENT

The Budget continues to support the Administration's work to modernize Government for the 21st Century. The President's Management Agenda (PMA), launched in March 2018, set out a strategic vision for modernizing the Federal Government to improve mission outcomes, service to the people, and stewardship of taxpayer dollars.

Taxpayers expect their Federal Government to deliver citizen services in an effective and cost-efficient manner. Doing so requires a skilled workforce with timely access to relevant market information, business intelligence, and related data. The PMA advances a number of key drivers of change—including technology, data, and the workforce—and promotes coordination across agencies.

As the two-year anniversary of the PMA approaches, the Administration will continue to build toward a long-term vision of a Government that is responsive to the needs of the people it serves, agile in delivering on its mission, and responsible in its stewardship of taxpayer dollars. The next steps on the PMA will be released this spring. This chapter highlights specific success stories achieved by different teams through their PMA efforts, as well as some actions underway. Additional information on these initiatives and regular progress updates are available on *https://Performance.gov*.

IMPROVES EFFICIENCIES IN GOVERNMENT

Makes Government Leaner and More Efficient. In the Budget, Federal agencies have proposed elimination or modification of more than 500 plans and reports that are outdated or duplicative. Since the start of the Administration, the largest 24 Federal agencies have implemented more than 100 initiatives to reduce administrative burden and put more resources toward agency missions, driving billions of dollars in realized and anticipated savings and shifting hundreds of thousands of Full-Time Equivalent employee hours to higher-value work. These initiatives include more than 50 initiatives focused on process improvement and standardization; approximately 30 initiatives using robotic process automation, artificial intelligence, and/or other innovative software; and nearly 20 initiatives focused on the digitization of agency processes.

Aligns Federal Compensation with the Private Sector. The Congressional Budget Office (CBO) concluded in a series of recent reports that Federal employees are, on average, compensated with combined pay and benefits higher than the private sector. Most recently, in 2017, CBO found a 17-percent disparity on average, in total compensation, between Federal employees and their private sector peers. The disparity—which varies significantly by education level—is overwhelmingly attributable to benefits. CBO found that, in comparison to the private sector, the Federal Government continues to offer a very generous package of retirement benefits, even when controlling for certain characteristics of workers. To align Federal compensation with leading private sector practices, the Budget continues to propose reforms to Federal benefits including: 1) increasing employee contributions to the Federal Employees Retirement System (FERS) such that the employee and employer would each pay half the normal cost; 2) eliminating the FERS Cost-of-Living Adjustment (COLA) and reducing the Civil Service Retirement System COLA; 3) eliminating the Special Retirement Supplement; 4) changing the retirement calculation from the High-3 years to High-5 years; and 5) reducing the Thrift Savings Plan G Fund interest rate.

Saves Money with Category Management. The Federal Government spends over $350 billion on common goods and services every year. Through the category management initiative, the Administration has aggregated demand for common goods and services, leveraged innovative procurement strategies, and improved data analytics. As a result, the Administration has reduced duplicative contracts by 26 percent, increased contract dollars to small businesses, created opportunities for new entrants, avoided costs of $27 billion, and is on track to achieve $36 billion in savings by the end of 2020. The Budget includes resources to further support statutory and regulatory changes to leverage procurement data more strategically and reduce expensive friction in acquisitions.

Streamlines Review and Permitting for Major Infrastructure Projects. Major infrastructure projects are vital to American competitiveness and long-term economic growth, but the environmental review and permitting process has for too long been opaque, overly complex, and unpredictable for businesses and State and local partners. The Administration has instituted a new integrated, cross-agency approach to increase transparency, accountability, and efficiency for all stakeholders, resulting in over $1 billion in cost savings through avoided permitting delays.

Saves Taxpayer Time and Money with Shared Support Services. In 2019, the Administration established a whole-of-Government framework for improving service quality, eliminating duplicative efforts, leveraging the Government's buying power, and replacing antiquated technology. This new model delivers more value to American taxpayers by identifying, planning, and operating Government-wide shared services.

Manages Real Property Efficiently. The Administration has prioritized optimizing the Federal Real Property Portfolio to achieve the mission while minimizing cost. The *Analytical Perspectives* volume chapter 7, "Federal Real Property," describes recent accomplishments and the vision to achieve this reform.

Reorganizes Government. The Administration issued a bold reform and reorganization plan in June 2018 to build productive, bipartisan dialogue around realigning the Federal Government mission delivery model to better meet the needs of the 21st Century. Positive progress on these proposals includes the successful transfer of the background investigation mission from the Office of Personnel Management to the Department of Defense in October 2019. Improvements to business processes and expanded capacity have already reduced the investigation backlog by over 64 percent from 725,000 in April 2018 to under 261,000 in December 2019. The Budget builds on this success by proposing to transfer the United States Secret Service from the Department of Homeland Security to the Department of the Treasury, which would result in enhancements to counterfeit and cybercrime investigations.

Prevents Improper Payments. Preventing improper payments that result in a monetary loss is a high priority for the Administration. Government-wide efforts leverage risk-based approaches that improve payment accuracy and increase access to data and mitigation strategies for agencies, State governments, and the public to help detect, prevent, and recover improper payments. The Administration has identified a suite of proposals, detailed in the Budget, that would save $182 billion over 10 years, if enacted. For additional details, please refer to the *Analytical Perspectives* volume chapter 6, "Payment Integrity," which includes Budget proposals aimed at preventing these improper payments.

Improves Acquisitions in the Digital Age. Modernizing the Federal acquisition system for the digital age requires the development of tactical strategies and practical tools that support improved access to business intelligence, as well as the accelerated identification, testing, and adoption of meaningful changes to business practices. To accelerate the pace of modernization, the Administration will baseline the current state of acquisition innovation, pilot a centralized information sharing knowledge management resource, promote emerging technologies, and scale application of a proven model to coach innovative practices.

DEVELOPS A MORE RESPONSIVE GOVERNMENT

Improves Customer Experience. The Administration recognizes every interaction between the Federal Government and the public as an opportunity to demonstrate that Government is working to meet the public's needs. The PMA pushes Federal programs to view their work from the perspective and experience of the customer and align talent and resources accordingly. This year, for the first time, Federal agencies have shared their plans to improve the way they serve their customers, putting their new High Impact Service Providers' Customer Experience profiles online at *https://performance.gov*. By connecting the people with these plans, the Administration is increasing the transparency and accountability of 25 of the largest public-facing services in a ground-breaking way.

Accelerates Government Modernization. Since its launch in March 2019, the Technology Modernization Fund Board has awarded approximately $90 million to nine initiatives to accelerate modernization across the Government while demonstrating efficient management of taxpayer resources. In 2020, two new modernization projects have been approved to leverage innovative commercial capabilities to enable digital transformations and enhance the speed at which improved citizen services are delivered.

Engages Government with Private Sector. In September 2019, the Administration awarded almost $1 million to three teams of diverse collaborators through the Government Effectiveness Advanced Research Center challenge competition. These teams will demonstrate how Government can catch up to private-sector services and capabilities and will lay the groundwork for where operations and services need to be in 5, 10, and even 20 years.

Moves Government Closer to the People it Serves. The Administration successfully relocated the headquarters of the Bureau of Land Management (BLM) to Grand Junction, Colorado, where leadership will be closer to the 245 million acres of BLM-managed land in 11 western States and Alaska.

Leverages Data as a Strategic Asset. The world is creating data faster than ever before, with 90 percent of the data on the Internet created since 2016. Data from Federal programs should be used as a strategic asset to grow the economy, facilitate oversight, and promote transparency. After a year and a half of work and input from hundreds of stakeholders, the Administration released the *Federal Data Strategy 2020 Action Plan*, a significant milestone in the effort to create a coordinated approach to Federal data use and management that serves the public.

Uses Evidence to Promote Better Outcomes. The Administration continues to implement evidence-building activities to improve policy, programs, and regulations, including through multiyear learning agendas, annual evaluation plans, and capacity assessments.

INCREASES AGILITY FOR A MORE MODERN GOVERNMENT

Improves Federal Hiring. The Administration is piloting a new way to assess qualifications for applicants to the competitive service, with the goal of ensuring only qualified candidates make it to hiring managers for review, particularly in positions of highly technical or specialized knowledge. On the heels of the success of these initial pilots, the Administration codified "Subject Matter Expert Qualification Assessments," and is prototyping technology to engage subject matter experts in new assessments for specialized human capital recruitments.

Addresses the Federal Cybersecurity Shortage. A cyber reskilling pilot program offers Federal employees the opportunity for hands-on training in cybersecurity, one of the fastest growing fields in the Nation and critical to protecting Government data from bad actors. These projects demonstrate a path forward for reskilling Federal employees to achieve and sustain needed skills inside the Federal workforce.

Secures the National Supply Chain. In 2019, as part of the National Cyber Strategy and the SECURE Technology Act, agencies were required to assess the risks to their respective information and communications technology supply chains. The Administration established the Federal Acquisition Security Council to help agencies safeguard information and communication technology from emerging threats and support the need to establish standards for the acquisition community with respect to supply chain risk management.

Promotes Results-Oriented Accountability for Grants. The Federal Government has over 1,400 grant programs and over 28 grant-making agencies. By centralizing the collection of grants data, the Administration is saving grantees over 150,000 work hours annually. Less time on red tape means more time turning grant dollars into results for the American taxpayer. The PMA supports new standard data elements that set the stage for future grants management shared solutions and policies to reduce administrative burden, promote transparency, and increase return on taxpayer investment. The *Analytical Perspectives* volume chapter 14, "Aid to State and Local Governments," describes the vision to achieve this reform.

Improves Management of Acquisitions. In 2019, the Administration took steps to establish an official career path for program managers to ensure they are appropriately trained and certified to collaborate with contracting officials in managing major acquisitions. Agencies also created and strengthened structures to manage similar investments in their portfolios and identified priority projects for heightened management attention.

Strengthens Performance and Risk Management. The Administration continues to leverage best practices from across sectors to drive organizational performance improvement and better risk management. In quarterly performance reviews for the 85 Agency Priority Goals (APGs) for 2018-2019, the overwhelming majority met or exceeded their performance targets. With the release of the Budget, agencies have set over 90 new APGs for the coming two years. Agencies and the Office of Management and Budget will continue to use Strategic Reviews in 2020 to assess programs and major risks to over 300 mission objectives. To further support the maturity of Enterprise Risk Management (ERM), the Administration established an Executive Steering Committee that will identify and share best practices, assess maturity of ERM programs, promote ERM integration within mission and mission support functions, and facilitate constructive coordination with oversight entities.

DEPARTMENT OF AGRICULTURE

Funding Highlights:

- The U.S. Department of Agriculture (USDA) provides leadership and direction on issues related to food, agriculture, and natural resources based on sound policy, the best available science, and effective management.

- The Budget for USDA focuses on core Departmental activities such as agricultural research, rural lending, and protecting the Nation's forested and private agricultural lands, while also supporting the President's efforts to give American farmers and ranchers the tools they need to be competitive at home and abroad.

- The Budget eliminates duplicative and wasteful programs within the Rural Business Service which gives funds to businesses that could qualify for private sector capital, saving $91 million from the 2020 enacted level.

- The 2021 Budget requests $21.8 billion in discretionary resources for USDA, a $1.9 billion or 8-percent decrease from the 2020 enacted level. The Budget proposes $240 billion in net mandatory savings over 10 years from USDA programs to reduce long-term deficits.

The President's 2021 Budget:

USDA's broad mission encompasses everything from domestic food assistance programs in rural America, to farm loans, and the National Forest System. Throughout rural America, USDA's programs provide financing for farm operations as well as improve rural utilities and infrastructure needed to keep America's commodities moving to market. The Department works to promote agricultural production while also safeguarding and protecting America's food supply by reducing the incidence of food-borne hazards through the inspection of meat, poultry, and egg products.

The Department's programs also improve nutrition and health through food assistance and nutrition education. Under this Administration, the Supplemental Nutrition Assistance Program (SNAP) has been streamlined to remove eligibility loopholes and improve program integrity, ensuring benefits are appropriately targeted to those most in need. USDA works to increase foreign market access for U.S. agricultural products and provides data and analysis of foreign market conditions. In addition, USDA manages and protects America's public and private lands by working cooperatively across the Government and the private sector to preserve and conserve the Nation's natural resources through restored forests, improved watersheds, and healthy private working lands.

Stands with America's Farmers. Farmers are experiencing high levels of financial stress due to challenging market and growing conditions. To help farmers survive the market shocks, the Administration has provided $28 billion in trade mitigation assistance and $5.7 billion in supplemental and ad hoc disaster assistance. This unprecedented level of support underscores the President's commitment to the Nation's farmers and ranchers. In total, roughly one-third of farm income will come from Government payments and crop insurance benefits this year. As a result, USDA is projecting that farm income will rise for the third year in a row, and if projections are realized, farm income would be above the historical average of the 2000 to 2018 period.

> *"[W]e will ensure that our farmers get the relief they need and very, very quickly. It's a good time to be a farmer; we're going to make sure of that."*
>
> President Donald J. Trump
> May 23, 2019

In addition to funding the robust suite of farm safety net programs, the Budget funds a variety of national, State, and local initiatives to help farmers succeed. At the national level, the Budget funds training for field office staff to provide support to farmers participating in USDA programs. The Budget also provides nearly $7 million to help farmers and ranchers resolve financial disputes related to USDA farm loans, conservation programs, and other issues. The Budget also proposes $2 million in research funding for farm business management grants and $8 million to support the Farmer Stress Assistance Extension Network.

Combats Opioid Crisis. According to the Centers for Disease Control and Prevention, the rates of drug overdose deaths are rising in rural communities, surpassing the rate in urban areas. Through the President's leadership and the role of the Secretary as Chairman of the Task Force on Agriculture and Rural Prosperity, the Department is approaching the opioid crisis with a dedicated urgency by partnering with local communities to provide program resources for prevention, treatment, and recovery. The Budget proposes $44 million in distance learning and telemedicine grants, of which 20 percent would be dedicated to projects that combat the opioid crisis and keep rural communities safe.

Reforms Food Stamp Program to Promote Work. The Budget continues bold proposals to reform work requirements for able-bodied adults participating in SNAP to promote self-sufficiency. This proposal would streamline SNAP work requirements and apply them consistently to able-bodied adults ages 18 to 65, unless they qualify for specific exemptions. Under the proposal, adults would be required to work, participate in job training, or volunteer at least 20 hours a week in order to receive SNAP benefits. The Budget also combines the traditional SNAP Electronic Benefits Transfer benefits with "Harvest Boxes" of 100 percent American-grown foods provided directly to households, ensuring that Americans in need have access to a nutritious diet while significantly reducing the cost to taxpayers. States would maintain the ability to provide choice to their participants, including by using innovative approaches for the inclusion of fresh products. To bolster State program integrity initiatives, the Budget provides for the nationwide implementation of the National Accuracy Clearinghouse, an interstate data-matching system to prevent duplicate participation in SNAP. The Budget also includes proposals to reserve benefits for those most in need, promote efficiency in State operations, and strengthen program monitoring and oversight.

Prioritizes Health Outcomes for Pregnant Women, Infants, and Young Children. The Budget requests $5.5 billion to serve all projected participants in the Special Supplemental Nutrition program for Women, Infants, and Children. This program provides nutritious supplemental food packages, nutrition education, and health and immunization referrals to low-income and nutritionally at-risk pregnant and postpartum women, infants, and children.

Invests in Rural America. In today's information-driven global economy, e-connectivity has become an essential component to attract and grow rural businesses. To that end, the Budget supports continued implementation of the Rural e-Connectivity Pilot Program to foster thriving agricultural economies. The Department also helps to maintain and modernize rural utilities by providing critical support for infrastructure, such as $614 million in funding for water and wastewater grants and loans, supporting $1.9 billion in program level, $5.5 billion in electric loans, and $690 million in telecommunications loans. Through USDA's $24 billion portfolio of guaranteed housing loans, the Department assists lenders in providing low- to moderate-income rural Americans with access to affordable housing. The Budget authorizes a $2.5 billion loan level for community facility direct loans and $500 million for guaranteed loans, which assist communities in developing or improving essential public services and facilities across rural America, such as health clinics or fire and rescue stations.

At the same time, the Budget reduces wasteful spending within the Rural Business Service by eliminating ineffective programs and instead supporting a $1.5 billion loan level for business and industry guaranteed loans, an increase of $500 million over the 2020 enacted level and offset through increased lending fees.

Supports Comprehensive Farm Safety Net Reforms and Reduces Waste. Building on the agricultural reforms proposed in the 2020 Budget, the Administration continues proposals to modify and target crop insurance, conservation, and commodity programs in a way that maintains a strong safety net, saving $36 billion over 10 years. The Budget also proposes to eliminate wasteful duplication and excessive subsidies between federally subsidized crop insurance and mandatory disaster assistance. This addresses recent congressional changes that removed safeguards and would ensure that taxpayer funded assistance is limited and that producers do not collect more than 100 percent for the same loss.

Safeguards Agricultural Research. USDA funded research helps to protect, secure, and improve America's food, agricultural, and natural resource systems. The Budget prioritizes competitive research through the Department's flagship grant program, the Agriculture and Food Research Initiative (AFRI). The Budget requests $600 million for AFRI, an increase of $175 million above the 2020 enacted level. Industries of the future are major Administration Research and Development priorities in 2021, such as artificial intelligence (AI) that has significant potential to contribute to U.S. scientific leadership and economic competitiveness in agriculture. That is why $100 million in AFRI funding would be targeted toward basic and applied research in AI. The Budget maintains formula-based research and extension grants at the level requested in the 2020 Budget. The Budget supports the Administration's initiative to promote excellence and innovation at Historically Black Colleges and Universities by including $10 million for scholarships for students studying agriculture at historically black land-grant institutions. The Budget proposes $1.3 billion for the Agricultural Research Service, which conducts in-house basic and applied research. This includes funding for the National Bio- and Agro-Defense Facility, currently near completion in Manhattan, Kansas. This state of the art facility will provide the United States the ability to conduct comprehensive research, develop vaccines, and provide enhanced diagnostic capabilities to protect against emerging foreign animal and zoonotic diseases that threaten the Nation's food supply, agricultural economy, and public health.

Supports Active Forest Management to Reduce Wildfire Risk. The Administration remains committed to accelerating active forest management activities. The Budget reflects this critical priority by requesting $510 million for hazardous fuel mitigation work and $385 million for forest products. Hazardous fuel removal is pivotal in ensuring Federal forests and watersheds are sustainable, healthy, and productive, which would help make them safer and more resilient to the destructive impacts of wildfire. Consistent with the objectives and targets under the President's Executive Order 13855, "Promoting Active Management of America's Forests, Rangelands, and other Federal Lands to

Improve Conditions and Reduce Wildfire Risk," the Forest Service will utilize the full range of available and appropriate forest management tools, including prescribed burns and mechanical thinning to strategically mitigate the fuel load on national forest land. These programs also generate jobs in rural forest communities.

In addition, the Budget fully funds base wildfire suppression operations pursuant to the Consolidated Appropriations Act, 2018, which would be bolstered by $2.4 billion in additional suppression resources under the wildfire cap adjustment. This funding aims to eliminate the need for disruptive "fire borrowing" from forest management programs to fund firefighting shortfalls during times of emergency.

Updates Customer Service. The Budget supports the continued modernization of USDA's information technology with investments made to improve customer service and streamline rural and farm program and service delivery. Through the *https://Farmers.gov* service portal, USDA is continuously working toward greater online service delivery with the goal of fewer in-person and paper-based transactions. The Budget continues to support farm production and conservation assistance by improving the efficiency, effectiveness, and accountability in service delivery between the Farm Service Agency, Natural Resources Conservation Service, and Risk Management Agency.

DEPARTMENT OF COMMERCE

Funding Highlights:

- The Department of Commerce (DOC) promotes job creation and economic growth. The Department ensures fair and reciprocal trade, provides the data necessary to support commerce and constitutional democracy, protects intellectual property, and fosters innovation by setting standards and conducting foundational research and development.

- The Budget request for DOC prioritizes and protects investments in core Government functions such as completing the 2020 Decennial Census, providing the observational infrastructure to produce timely and accurate weather forecasts, and enforcing laws that promote fair and secure trade.

- The Budget eliminates the Economic Development Administration (EDA) which provides hundreds of small grants for projects with limited measurable impacts, saving taxpayers $300 million per year. The projects use taxpayer dollars on multiyear projects that frequently fail to deliver on promised jobs or private investment.

- The 2021 Budget requests $7.9 billion for DOC, a $7.3 billion or 48.0-percent decrease from the 2020 enacted level, including changes in mandatory programs.

The President's 2021 Budget:

DOC has one overarching purpose, to help the American economy grow. Spurring innovation is a key driver of economic advancement, and as such the Budget invests in industries of the future, such as artificial intelligence (AI) and next generation communications technologies. The Budget also helps keep American people and property safe by maintaining the capabilities necessary to provide warnings for extreme weather and disruptive solar events. U.S. businesses deserve the most accurate statistical and scientific data to prosper in an increasingly competitive world, and look to DOC to enforce trade laws to ensure that trade is free, fair, and reciprocal. The Budget invests in these critical functions while cutting unnecessary programs that do not work for the American taxpayer.

Focuses on Industries of the Future. The Budget provides $718 million for the National Institute of Standards and Technology (NIST) to advance U.S. innovation and technological development, as part of an all-of-Government approach to ensure that the United States leads the world in the areas of AI, quantum information science, advanced manufacturing, and next generation communications technologies such as 5G. The Budget doubles NIST's AI funding, in order to accelerate the development and adoption of AI technologies and help ensure AI-enabled systems are interoperable,

"Secure 5G networks will absolutely be a vital link to America's prosperity and national security in the 21ˢᵗ Century. 5G will be as much as 100 times faster than the current 4G cellular networks. It will transform the way our citizens work, learn, communicate, and travel. It will make American farms more productive, American manufacturing more competitive, and American healthcare better and more accessible. Basically, it covers almost everything, when you get right down to it. Pretty amazing."

President Donald J. Trump
April 12, 2019

secure, and reliable. The Budget also proposes the creation of a second NIST-funded advanced manufacturing institute to collaborate with industry and ensure that innovations developed in the United States are also manufactured in the United States rather than in other countries. In addition, the Budget prepares for the future by providing the National Telecommunications and Information Administration with $25 million to modernize spectrum management systems, enabling the United States to more efficiently satisfy industry's need for additional spectrum, and preparing the Nation to transition to 5G.

Prioritizes Free and Fair Trade. The Budget includes an additional $10 million to support the President's robust trade agenda in order to protect critical elements of U.S economic security and level the playing field for American workers, farmers, and manufacturers. The Budget supports ongoing efforts to identify and protect emerging and foundational technologies that are essential to national security and economic prosperity. The Budget also provides additional resources to ensure the timely review of exclusion requests from Section 232 tariffs. These efforts ensure that the U.S. steel and aluminum industries are protected, but that U.S. industry can access materials that are critical for U.S. national security.

Supports 2020 Census. In 2021, the Decennial Census will enter its final phase. Following a decade of planning and execution, the Census Bureau will ramp down the massive coordination of people and infrastructure that supported the 2020 Decennial Census. The Bureau will release data used to redistrict congressional seats and make decisions about Federal funding.

Maintains Critical Weather Satellite Funding. Businesses, communities, governments, and the general public rely on satellite data and products to provide reliable, accurate information on which to make decisions regarding public safety and emergency preparedness. The Budget provides $1.2 billion in funding to maintain satellites in polar and geostationary orbits for weather prediction, and in deep space to provide data used to generate warnings for damaging solar events. Notably, the Budget provides $108 million to continue development of the Space Weather Follow On (SWFO) mission. This funding would allow the SWFO satellite to stay on schedule and launch with a National Aeronautics and Space Administration research mission, thereby eliminating the need for an additional launch which would lead to better stewardship of taxpayer dollars. The Budget also provides nearly $50 million to create a more efficient and effective satellite architecture of the future, with targeted investments in commercial satellite data and new capabilities to enable the next generation of weather satellites.

Spurs Innovation through Ocean Mapping. The President signed the Memorandum on Ocean Mapping of the United States Exclusive Economic Zone and the Shoreline and Nearshore of Alaska on November 19, 2019. The U.S. exclusive economic zone (EEZ) is among the largest in the world and is larger than the combined land area of all fifty States; the ocean economy produces more than $300 billion in goods and services annually. However, because only about 40 percent of the U.S. EEZ has been mapped, the United States lacks critical data that could support and inform economic development and new scientific discoveries. In addition, Alaska and the Alaskan Arctic lack the comprehensive shoreline and nearshore maps available to much of the Nation. In support of this Memorandum, the Budget provides $188 million to continue efforts at the National Oceanic and Atmospheric Administration (NOAA) to map and explore the U.S. EEZ and Alaska, as well as support existing navigation and mapping programs. This additional mapping and research would improve the Nation's understanding of the vast resources in the oceans, and identify new sources of critical minerals, biopharmaceuticals, and energy, and areas of significant ecological and conservation value.

Improves the Delivery of America's Economic Statistics. The President and the Administration are improving a once-stagnant economy with pro-growth policies, and the Nation's economic data tells the story of this success. The Budget recognizes the importance of economic statistics for businesses and everyday citizens to make informed decisions and confidently invest in America's future. Further, as part of the Administration's commitment to deploying Government resources to the neediest communities more effectively, the Budget provides funding to improve poverty measurement in America.

The Administration urges the Congress to favorably consider the *Delivering Government Solutions in the 21st Century* plan's recommendation to consolidate within DOC critical economic statistics programs at the Census Bureau, the Bureau of Economic Analysis, and the Bureau of Labor Statistics. This consolidation would make agency operations more efficient, improve products, and reduce the burden on respondents, while preserving the Agencies' brand recognition and independence.

Eliminates Wasteful and Duplicative Programs. Increased spending is a threat to the Nation's future and accordingly, the Budget eliminates unnecessary programs in order to prioritize the essential functions of the U.S. Government. The Budget eliminates EDA, which has negligible measureable impacts and duplicates other Federal programs. Many of EDA's programs have not been authorized by the Congress for decades and multiple administrations have called for their reform. Examples of wasteful spending include spending on a National Comedy Center in Jamestown, New York, and a cosmetology institute in Las Vegas, Nevada, an area that already has 17 similar schools. Eliminating this program saves taxpayers $300 million per year.

The Budget also discontinues Federal funding for the Manufacturing Extension Partnership, recognizing that the program should transition to non-Federal funding as originally intended when the program was established.

The Budget proposes elimination of funding for several lower priority NOAA programs, including Sea Grant, Coastal Zone Management Grants, Education Grants, and the Pacific Coastal Salmon Recovery Fund. These grant programs generally support State, local, and/or industry interests, and often are not optimally targeted. For example, some of these grants have supported activities such as local tourism efforts and rain garden education and installation, both of which are more appropriately funded at the local level.

DEPARTMENT OF DEFENSE

Funding Highlights:

- The Department of Defense (DOD) provides the combat-credible military forces and capabilities needed to deter aggression, fight and win wars, and protect the security of the United States.

- The 2021 Budget delivers on the President's promise to rebuild America's military, strengthen readiness for the future, and support the Nation's warfighters. The Budget implements the 2018 National Defense Strategy by prioritizing essential investments in modernization, lethality, and innovation that provide the U.S military with the required capabilities to meet current and future challenges.

- The Budget reflects the Administration's commitment to streamline bureaucracy, ensure good stewardship of taxpayer dollars, and prioritize the core functions of Government. As part of this effort, the Budget supports DOD's comprehensive review of defense-wide organizations, known as DOD's Fourth Estate, which identified over $5 billion in savings in 2021 and transferred an additional $2 billion in activities and functions to the military departments for more effective and efficient operations. The effort reduces Office of the Secretary of Defense programs and reinvests savings in innovation and lethality initiatives that would strengthen the U.S. military's competitive advantage in high-end warfare.

- The Budget requests $705.4 billion for DOD, including $636.4 billion for the base budget and $69 billion for Overseas Contingency Operations (OCO). The Budget reflects a $0.8 billion increase above the 2020 enacted level for base and OCO.

The President's 2021 Budget:

The Budget provides the necessary resources for DOD to protect and defend the homeland, maintain balances of power in key regions of strategic importance, and exert a sphere of influence that supports U.S. security and prosperity. Ultimately, the Budget reflects the President's commitment to ensure America's military remains second to none, both today and into the future.

Underpinned by the 2018 National Defense Strategy, the Budget sustains and builds on efforts over the last three years to prioritize investments in modernization, lethality, and innovation that provide the Nation's warfighters a competitive advantage against growing threats from near-peer adversaries, such as China and Russia; deter aggressive regional challengers; and maintain pressure on terrorist groups throughout the world. The Budget continues the Administration's work to rebuild the military and improve readiness, while balancing the need for reform, efficiency, and accountability at every level.

> *"Together, the men and women of America's Armed Forces are the most extraordinary warriors ever to walk the face of the Earth. You stand ready to vanquish any danger and deliver the full might of American justice whenever and wherever duty calls."*
>
> President Donald J. Trump
> June 30, 2019

The Budget supports U.S. military dominance in all warfighting domains—air, land, sea, space, and cyberspace. Essential funding is provided to research, design, and procure advanced capabilities across each of the services, including 115 modern fighter aircraft, modernization of one armored brigade combat team per year, and a total of 10 battle force and unmanned ships. The Budget supports U.S. technical superiority by investing in innovative, crosscutting programs such as artificial intelligence, microelectronics, and hypersonic weapons. Further, the Budget supports a total military end strength of 2,153,500 active duty and reserve personnel, including personnel to grow America's newest military Service, the United States Space Force (USSF). Most importantly, the Budget puts the needs of the warfighter and their families first with a 3.0-percent increase in military basic pay.

Invests in Modernization and Lethality

Ensures Maritime Superiority. The Budget sustains the Administration's emphasis on growing the world's most advanced and lethal naval force by investing $19.3 billion to procure a total of 10 new battle force and unmanned ships, including funding the recapitalization of the strategic ballistic missile submarine (SSBN) fleet with *Columbia*-class SSBNs. The Budget prioritizes funding for programs that would deliver warfighting advantages against China and Russia, including high-end extended range munitions, unmanned systems, hypersonic and advanced strike missiles, directed energy, containerized weapons, and information warfare capabilities. In addition, the Budget balances the need to maintain readiness with investments in future growth to ensure America's naval forces are prepared to protect and defend national interests anywhere in the world.

Grows the USSF. Building on its historic establishment in the previous budget, the Budget supports the growth of the USSF to ensure it can advance America's national interests in space. The Budget provides $111 million to fund essential personnel growth for the USSF, including staff for centers for development of doctrine, testing, and training for the new Service. The USSF is realigning existing space forces and materiel from the Air Force in the near term and scaling up with other components over the next several years in order to address increasing threats and maintain strategic advantage. The Budget also grows the Space Development Agency, which was established in 2019 to foster innovation by leveraging the thriving domestic commercial space sector, and the U.S. Space Command, which would employ the forces and capabilities of the USSF.

Strengthens U.S. Missile Defeat and Defense. The Budget provides $20.3 billion to strengthen missile defeat and defense programs. To advance the 2019 Missile Defense Review's policy of providing effective and enduring protection against rogue state missile threats to the homeland, the Budget proposes additional investments in more robust Homeland Missile Defense programs. Specifically, the Budget proposes assessing the potential modification of existing regional missile defense programs for layered homeland defense, some of which can be demonstrated as early as 2025.

Prioritizes Nuclear Deterrence. America's nuclear deterrent is the backstop and foundation of the Nation's defense and that of America's allies. To address the return of great power competition and implement the Administration's 2018 Nuclear Posture Review, the Budget continues investments in modernizing critical nuclear delivery systems. The Budget also supports the critical ongoing enhancement of the Nation's Nuclear Command, Control, and Communications system.

Delivers Airpower for the Future Fight. The Budget prioritizes funding for programs that would deliver the U.S. airpower needed to prevail in the highly contested fights of the future. The Budget invests $15.1 billion in DOD's tactical fighter programs, continuing the procurement of F-35A stealth fighters and new, upgraded, F-15EX fighter aircraft for the Air Force, and the procurement of the Navy's and Marine Corps' variants of the F-35. The Budget also modernizes the Navy's current F/A-18E/F fighters and accelerates the development of the next generation of advanced fighter aircraft. Funding supports the development of the new stealth bomber and the procurement of the KC-46 aerial refueling tanker. These mission critical investments would ensure that DOD can successfully counter the wide variety of threats that are expected in future air combat situations.

Improves Ground Combat Lethality. The Budget provides significant funding to improve the lethality of ground combat capabilities, including nearly $11 billion to fund modernization of long-range precision artillery, combat vehicles and helicopters, command and control networks, air and missile defense, and close combat training and equipment. The Budget also provides over $3 billion to support the modernization of one armored brigade combat team per year. Further, the Budget prioritizes the development of next generation combat systems over the sustainment of Cold War-era legacy platforms to deliver greater firepower for high intensity combat.

Funds Leading Edge Innovation

Ensures Technological Superiority by Investing in Industries of the Future. The Budget supports critical investments to regain and sustain U.S. technological superiority to counter and overmatch emerging threats. The Budget invests over $14 billion in DOD science and technology programs that support key investments in industries of the future, such as artificial intelligence, quantum information science, and biotechnology, as well as core DOD modernization priorities such as hypersonic weapons, directed energy, 5G, space, autonomy, microelectronics, cybersecurity, and fully-networked command, control, and communications.

Accelerates Development of Offensive Hypersonic Weapons. DOD continues to accelerate the development and demonstration of offensive hypersonic weapon capabilities. The Budget provides $3.2 billion, $459 million more than the 2020 enacted level, to continue development of Army, Navy, and Air Force weapons variants. In addition, the Budget supports increased operational flight testing necessary to accelerate delivery of fully operational weapon systems that would provide unprecedented offensive strike capability across multiple warfighting domains.

Ensures Access to Trusted and Assured Microelectronics. The Budget invests in necessary enhancements to ensure that the United States can maintain trusted and reliable access to state-of-the-art microelectronics suppliers. The Budget enables secure design, development, fabrication, and assembly of microelectronics without the need to invest in a costly Government-owned and operated fabrication facility. These investments are essential for the development of next generation capabilities in communications, computing, artificial intelligence, and autonomy.

Invests in Cyber Capability. The Budget builds on progress in recent years to develop the military's cyber capabilities by requesting nearly $10 billion in 2021. The cyber budget is aligned to advance DOD's three primary cyber missions: safeguarding DOD's networks, information, and systems; supporting military commander objectives; and defending the Nation. This investment provides the resources necessary to grow the capacity of U.S. military cyber forces, including U.S. Cyber Command, invest in the cyber workforce, and continue to maintain the highest cybersecurity standards at DOD.

Maximizes Readiness and Supports the Warfighter

Puts the Warfighter First. People are the Department's most valuable asset. Providing a robust pay and benefits package is imperative to ensure that DOD remains best positioned to compete with the private sector for new recruits and that DOD can retain a well-trained volunteer force. The Budget proposes a 3.0-percent increase in military basic pay and provides funding for a full range of important compensation programs to support America's servicemembers and their families. The Budget also grows military end-strength by over 13,000 from 2020 authorized levels to enable the services to continue to improve readiness, while addressing critical capability gaps.

Sustains and Builds on Readiness Gains. The Budget sustains and accelerates readiness gains across each of the services in recent years as a result of the Administration's focus on rebuilding the military. The Budget provides an increase of $1.4 billion for the Navy's ship and aircraft operations and maintenance accounts to significantly reduce the surface ship and submarine maintenance backlog, while ensuring that Navy and Marine Corps aircraft mission capable rates continue to improve. For the Air Force, the Budget optimizes resources by redirecting funding for combat flying hours, weapons sustainment, and training from aging, legacy aircraft to next generation platforms and systems designed for the high-end fight, such as the F-35 joint strike fighter and KC-46 aerial refueling tanker. In addition, for the Army, the Budget emphasizes readiness-generating activities tied directly to the National Defense Strategy, such as large-scale training activities in Europe and Asia as well as enhancing tactical proficiency within operational forces.

Divests Legacy Systems to Ensure Readiness Tomorrow. The Budget supports DOD's effort to divest $20 billion of legacy systems over the Future Years Defense Program (FYDP) in order to reallocate resources in support of the National Defense Strategy. By shedding older and less capable aircraft, surface ships, and ground systems, DOD can more effectively focus resources to modernized platforms and systems that support both high-intensity conflict and operations in highly contested environments.

Maintains Pressure on Terrorist Groups while Focusing on Great Power Competition. The Budget maintains the funding necessary to continue DOD counterterrorism efforts to ensure terrorists do not have the capacity to attack the U.S. homeland or America's allies. Building on trends from the previous budget, the Budget further implements the 2018 National Defense Strategy by prioritizing programs and efforts that are necessary to prepare for the high-end fight. The Budget de-emphasizes funding in areas that support operations in U.S. Central Command, while furthering the shift in resources toward great power competition efforts in the European and Indo-Pacific Commands.

Promotes Reform, Efficiency, and Accountability

Achieves Savings across the Department. The Budget reflects the Administration's commitment to ensuring good stewardship of taxpayer dollars by prioritizing resources for lethality and readiness initiatives. The Budget supports the Department's comprehensive review of DOD's Fourth Estate to ensure alignment with the National Defense Strategy and free up time, money, and manpower to reinvest in the Department's highest priorities. As part of this effort, known as the Defense-Wide Review, DOD identified over $5 billion in savings in 2021 to reallocate toward higher strategic priorities. The review also transferred an additional $2 billion in activities and functions to the military departments for more effective and efficient operations. The Budget reduces most DOD offices outside the military departments by at least five percent in an effort to counter defense-wide programs' growing share of the total DOD budget. The effort seeks to restore the appropriate balance between defense-wide organizations and the military departments, while promoting long-term structural reform of DOD's defense-wide activities.

Reforms Business Operations for Greater Performance and Accountability. DOD continues to pursue management reforms to increase affordability and redirect savings to higher priorities. For example, DOD will continue to modernize and eliminate legacy business systems and processes to reduce duplication, which will yield significant savings. In 2019, the Department achieved reform savings totaling $6 billion. In 2020 DOD is on track to achieve $7.7 billion in savings and nearly $45 billion across the FYDP. DOD's reform efforts include initiatives to sunset legacy data systems, transfer personnel data infrastructure to cloud technology, and transition legacy information technology infrastructure to emerging capabilities. DOD will continue to seek new ways to do business by leveraging the results of the recently completed audit, and continuing annual audits to promote transparency and accountability. DOD's reforms will not only produce savings for the Department, but also improve processes to ensure DOD prioritizes support for the warfighter.

Implements Successful Background Investigation Mission Transfer. DOD will continue its mission of conducting background investigations for the Federal Government following the successful transfer from the Office of Personnel Management in 2019, a key pillar of the President's Management Agenda. The transfer will dramatically improve the ability of agencies to deliver mission outcomes, and will continue to provide economy of scale in addressing the Federal Government's background investigations workload. The Budget requests funding for critical technology protection associated with this mission, while eliminating the need for additional resources since these activities are funded via the Defense Counterintelligence and Security Agency Working Capital Fund.

Reforms the Military Health System. DOD will continue rightsizing the military medical force to meet the Department's medical obligations in support of the National Defense Strategy. In addition, the Department will complete the transition of management and operations of the military treatment facilities from the services' Surgeons General to the Defense Health Agency. These two actions, coupled with the continued investments in trauma courses, medical simulation training, the alignment of medical readiness funds to the services, and continued Electronic Health Record modernization enable a renewed focus on readiness for uniformed servicemembers while ensuring the delivery of safe, high-quality healthcare.

DEPARTMENT OF EDUCATION

Funding Highlights:

- The Department of Education's mission is to support States and school districts in their efforts to provide high-quality education to the Nation's most vulnerable students, streamline and simplify funding for college, and expand access to postsecondary options.

- The Budget includes a substantial increase for Career and Technical Education of nearly $900 million to strengthen America's workforce by providing access to high-quality vocational programs in every high school. The Budget also provides increased funding for Historically Black Colleges and Universities and programs that serve disadvantaged populations.

- The Budget consolidates 29 narrowly focused or duplicative elementary and secondary programs into a new $19.4 billion block grant to States. The new program would give States and school districts the flexibility to better meet the needs of their students and families, eliminating Federal intrusion into State and local education systems. While providing a significant investment to U.S. schools, this approach saves taxpayers nearly $4.7 billion.

- The Budget requests $66.6 billion for the Department of Education, a $5.6 billion or 7.8-percent decrease compared to the 2020 enacted level.

The President's 2021 Budget:

The Department of Education's top priority is to promote education freedom: freedom for students and parents to choose the schools that best meet their needs; freedom for States and school districts to decide how best to meet the needs of their students; and freedom to choose high-quality, affordable postsecondary options and career pathways that lead to fulfilling lives. The Budget promotes these goals while restoring fiscal discipline in discretionary spending. The Budget also reduces Federal burdens on State and local education and places a particularly strong focus on providing a path to good jobs. In addition, the Budget expands families' ability to choose high-quality educational options for their children. The Budget would increase competition and transparency, reduce student debt, and ensure that what students are learning matches the needs of emerging industries. By increasing accountability for institutions of higher education and helping students only borrow as much as they need, the Budget would help make higher education more affordable while protecting both students and taxpayers.

K-12 Education

The Budget request for elementary and secondary education demonstrates the Administration's commitment to providing States and school districts with the funding and autonomy necessary to enable all children to receive a high-quality education, while also acknowledging the powerful contributions that high-quality career and technical education can make to both individual attainment and economic prosperity.

Creates a New Elementary and Secondary Education for the Disadvantaged Block Grant. The Administration proposes to consolidate 29 formula and competitive grant programs into a $19.4 billion formula grant that would allow States and school districts to decide how best to use the Elementary and Secondary Education Act of 1965 (ESEA) funds to address local educational needs and improve outcomes for all students. This proposal builds on an important goal of the 2015 Every Student Succeeds Act to restore greater State and local control over education while maintaining key accountability and reporting requirements aimed at protecting students, supporting meaningful school improvement efforts, and giving parents the information they need to choose a high-quality education for their children. The consolidation of most ESEA programs into a single block grant, which would allocate funds through the same formulas used by the Title I Grants to Local Educational Agencies program, would significantly reduce the Federal role in education and allow the Department to reduce staffing and administrative costs over time.

Increases support for Career and Technical Education (CTE). To support the Administration's commitment to preparing students to succeed in today's competitive, rapidly changing economy, and answer the ever increasing needs of a booming economy, the Budget includes $2 billion for CTE State Grants. This substantial increase over the 2020 enacted level builds on the Strengthening Career and Technical Education for the 21st Century Act, which would help ensure that all of the Nation's high schools are able to offer high-quality CTE programs. The Budget also includes $90 million for CTE National Programs to support high-quality science, technology, engineering, and mathematics and computer science CTE programs. In addition, the Budget proposes to double the American Competiveness and Workforce Improvement Act of 1998 fee for the H-1B visa program and direct 15 percent of the revenues to CTE State Grants, which is estimated to provide more than $100 million in additional funding for this program.

> *"As States begin to think about their long-term career and technical education strategies, I would encourage them to continue to act boldly and break down the silos that exist between education and industry so that all students are prepared for the in-demand, high-paying jobs of today's economy and tomorrow's."*
>
> Betsy DeVos
> Secretary
> July 1, 2019

> *"To help support working parents, the time has come to pass school choice for America's children."*
>
> President Donald J. Trump
> February 5, 2019

Provides Education Freedom to Families and Students. Families must have the freedom to choose the best learning experience for their children. The Administration's Education Freedom Scholarships proposal would provide up to $5 billion annually in State-designed scholarship programs that could support a range of educational activities such as CTE, special education services, and tuition for private school. This proposal would make tremendous strides toward the goal of providing all students with the opportunity to receive a high-quality education and achieve future success.

Invests Significant Resources for Students with Disabilities. The Administration believes that all children, including children with disabilities, should have access to a high-quality education. The Budget invests nearly $13 billion in Individuals with Disabilities Education Act (IDEA) Part B Grants to States, an increase of $100 million compared to the 2020 enacted level. This increase would provide more resources for States to provide special education and related services for over seven million students with disabilities. In addition, the Budget continues to fund all other IDEA grant programs at the 2020 enacted levels.

Higher Education

The Budget addresses student debt and higher education costs while reducing the complexity of student financial aid. The Budget provides further protection to students and taxpayers by eliminating unlimited loans and providing institutions with tools to help borrowers manage their debt.

Supports Improvements to Historically Black Colleges and Universities (HBCUs). The Budget includes important investments to support improvements at HBCUs. In total, the Budget proposes $749 million in discretionary funding to support HBCUs. The Budget also includes a proposal to consolidate six programs into a single formula grant to institutions serving low-income and minority students, providing funds more institutions can count on, yielding program management efficiencies, and targeting funds to institutions that serve their students well. In addition, the Budget proposes to target $150 million to support science, technology, engineering, and mathematics activities at HBCUs and other institutions serving historically disadvantaged students located in Opportunity Zones. Further, the Budget supports the recently passed FUTURE Act, which provides $85 million in mandatory funding to HBCUs each year.

Protects Students and Taxpayers from Growing Student Loan Burden. The Budget protects students by eliminating default for impoverished borrowers and providing expedited loan forgiveness for undergraduate borrowers who make 15 years of responsible payments. In addition, the Budget protects graduate and parent borrowers from racking up crushing debt, often never repaid to taxpayers, by instituting sensible annual and lifetime loan limits. In addition, the Budget closes loopholes currently allowing high-earning graduate-degree holding borrowers to avoid repaying their student loans, leaving taxpayers holding the bag.

Expands Pell Grant Eligibility to Short-Term Programs and Incarcerated Students. The Budget provides greater access to higher education opportunities by expanding eligibility for Pell Grants, the foundation of financial aid for low- and moderate-income students, in two key ways: first, students would be able to use Pell Grants at high-quality, short-term programs to gain the skills to secure well-paying jobs in high-demand fields more quickly than traditional two-year or four-year degree programs; second, the Budget makes Pell Grants available to certain incarcerated students to improve employment outcomes, reduce recidivism, and facilitate their successful reentry to society.

Empowers States to Deliver Evidence-Based Postsecondary Preparation Programs. Given fiscal constraints and the statutory prohibition limiting the Department's ability to rigorously evaluate program effectiveness, the Budget proposes to restructure and streamline the TRIO, GEAR UP, and CAMP programs by consolidating them into a $950 million State formula grant. This innovative proposal would support evidence-based postsecondary preparation programs designed to help low-income students progress through the pipeline from middle school to postsecondary opportunities.

Reduces Burden, Expands Options, and Protects Free Speech

Overly burdensome regulatory requirements can adversely affect the Nation's ability to prepare students for the opportunities and challenges of the 21st Century.

Protects Free Speech on College Campuses. The Department continues to support free and open debate on college and university campuses. Colleges and universities that receive Federal research or education grants must adhere to the requirements of the First Amendment to the Constitution and all other requirements of Federal law.

Reforms Accreditation to Promote Innovation and Lower Costs. The accreditation process is meant to ensure academic quality in higher education, but it had become a burdensome, costly exercise that forced schools to comply with a narrow vision of education. The Department's regulations streamline and reduce unnecessary costs associated with accreditation to open up paths for innovative programs and improve outcomes.

Safeguards Students from Fraudulent Institutions. The borrower defense rule establishes a clear standard for discharging student loans of borrowers defrauded by their institutions, providing transparency to both students and institutions. The rule also fairly holds all institutions to clear standards of accountability and allows the Department of Education to respond quickly and decisively to early signs of financial instability.

Rescinds Gainful Employment Regulations that Restricted Student Choice. On July 1, 2019, the Department rescinded the burdensome Gainful Employment regulations. The regulations failed to equitably hold all institutions accountable for student outcomes.

Improves Services for Taxpayers

Reforms and Modernizes Federal Student Aid. The Budget supports the multiyear Next Generation Financial Services Environment effort to build the technology and operational components that support the Federal student aid programs including the development and implementation of a new loan servicing platform to improve service for all Federal student loan borrowers. The office of Federal Student Aid is currently working to consolidate all of its customer-facing websites into a single, user-friendly hub to complement a new mobile platform and give students, parents, and borrowers a seamless experience from application through repayment.

Prioritizes Evidence and Evaluation. The Department of Education has long been a leading agency in building and using evidence. The Budget sets aside funds for higher education evaluation, which would be integrated into the Department's broader learning agenda development for the first time.

Reduces Waste: Eliminates Ineffective or Redundant Programs.

The Budget eliminates wasteful funding for 11 programs and consolidates 29 elementary and secondary programs into a new block grant. Eliminated programs include Federal Supplemental Education Opportunity Grants, which duplicates Pell Grants but are less targeted on those who need the most help. The Budget also eliminates International Education programs, given that a number of other Federal agencies offer programs that are similar and potentially duplicative. The new elementary and secondary block grant removes Federal bureaucracy and gives States flexibility to fund their own priorities. Consolidated programs include narrowly focused competitive grants and programs that have not proven to improve student outcomes. Together these policies would decrease taxpayer costs by $6.4 billion. In addition, the Budget saves $500 million by eliminating Account Maintenance Fees, excessive payments to student loan guaranty agencies participating in the wasteful legacy Family Federal Education Loan Program as it winds down.

DEPARTMENT OF ENERGY

Funding Highlights:

- The mission of the Department of Energy (DOE) is to advance U.S. national security and economic growth through transformative science and technology innovations that promote affordable and reliable energy through market solutions, and meet U.S. nuclear security and environmental clean-up challenges.

- The 2021 Budget makes strategic investments to maintain global leadership in scientific and technological innovation, including basic research in support of the Administration's efforts to foster industries of the future. The Budget also supports aggressively modernizing the nuclear security enterprise that underpins the safety and security of Americans both at home and abroad.

- The Budget proposes to sell federally-owned and operated electricity assets, which would save an estimated $4.1 billion over 10 years. Selling these assets would encourage a more efficient allocation of economic resources and mitigate unnecessary risks to taxpayers.

- The 2021 Budget requests $35.4 billion for DOE, an 8.1-percent decrease from the 2020 enacted level of $38.5 billion.

The President's 2021 Budget:

The Budget for DOE reflects the critical role DOE has in promoting energy dominance and economic growth and in protecting the safety and security of the American people. The Budget enables advancement of American leadership in science and technology, a cornerstone to achieving these goals. American ingenuity combined with free-market capitalism can drive tremendous technological breakthroughs, leading to improvements in America's economy and environment. The Budget focuses resources on early-stage research and development (R&D) of energy technologies, where the Federal role is strongest, while addressing the need to support later-stage R&D in targeted areas where there are unique challenges. Emphasizing the appropriate role of the Federal Government ensures that taxpayer dollars are being effectively used while implementing fiscal discipline.

The Budget also addresses the challenges associated with developing and maintaining the Nation's nuclear arsenal, another keystone to achieving the goals of security and prosperity. The Budget ensures that the United States continues to secure nuclear and radiological materials worldwide against theft by those seeking to harm this Nation or its allies. The Budget also funds the modernization of nuclear weapons and ensures that the U.S. nuclear force remains superior in the world.

In addition, the Budget promotes continued progress on cleaning up sites contaminated from nuclear weapons production and nuclear energy R&D.

The Budget further protects taxpayers by eliminating costly, wasteful, or duplicative programs. The private sector has the primary role in taking risks to finance the deployment of commercially viable projects and Government's best use of taxpayer funding is in earlier stage R&D. As a result, the Budget proposes to eliminate: the Title XVII Innovative Technology Loan Guarantee Program; the Advanced Technology Vehicle Manufacturing Loan Program; the Tribal Energy Loan Guarantee Program; and the Advanced Research Projects Agency–Energy.

The Budget again proposes to repeal the Western Area Power Administration's borrowing authority that finances the construction of electricity transmission projects. Investments in transmission assets are best carried out by the private sector with appropriate market and regulatory incentives that support resiliency and reliability.

Advances the Industries of the Future. The Budget prioritizes accelerating artificial intelligence (AI) solutions as part of implementing the Administration's efforts to foster industries of the future. DOE's new Artificial Intelligence and Technology Office will be responsible for providing Department-wide guidance and oversight on AI and will perform a critical role in ensuring offices across the Department are on the cutting-edge of AI technology development and application. The Budget provides $5 million for this new office to enhance important AI R&D projects already underway. The office would also coordinate crosscutting, mission-relevant projects as part of DOE's broader support for AI investments. In addition, the office would align these investments with the Administration's industries of the future efforts and with the White House Office of Science and Technology Policy's AI strategic priorities.

Supports Cutting-Edge Basic Research. The Budget provides $5.8 billion for the Office of Science to continue its mission to focus on early-stage research, operate national laboratories, and continue high priority construction projects. Within this amount: $475 million is requested for Exascale computing to help secure the United States as a global leader in supercomputing; $237 million is requested for quantum information science; $125 million is requested for AI and machine learning; and $45 million is requested to enhance materials and chemistry foundational research to support U.S.-based leadership in microelectronics.

Maintains a Safe, Secure, and Effective Nuclear Weapons Stockpile. The Budget for DOE's National Nuclear Security Administration (NNSA) supports the Administration's Nuclear Posture Review (NPR) by maintaining and modernizing the nuclear deterrent. The Nation's nuclear stockpile must be robust and effective to protect the homeland, assure allies, and deter adversaries. Specifically, the Budget continues investments to extend the life of warheads in the stockpile and modernize the supporting infrastructure.

Strengthens Nuclear Security Science, Technology, and Engineering Capabilities. The Budget maintains unique scientific capabilities at NNSA's national security laboratories, which provide the backbone of the science-based Stockpile Stewardship Program and enable NNSA and the Department of Defense to assess for the President that the Nation's nuclear weapons stockpile remains safe, secure, and effective without the need for nuclear explosive testing.

Prevents, Counters, and Responds to Global Nuclear Threats. Nuclear threats are constantly evolving, and the Budget for NNSA addresses these threats through integrated, coordinated efforts. The Budget increases funding for NNSA's national technical nuclear forensics capabilities, recognizing NNSA's key role in the NPR-required mission, and continues efforts to prevent terrorists from acquiring nuclear materials by removing materials from around the world and helping countries protect remaining materials.

Provides Reliable and Secure Nuclear Propulsion Systems for the U.S. Navy. The Budget continues DOE's support of a strong U.S. Navy through NNSA's Naval Reactors (NR) program. NR works to provide the U.S. Navy with safe, reliable operation of nuclear propulsion plants for submarines and aircraft carriers, including through the development of reactor systems for the *Columbia*-class ballistic missile submarine. The Budget also eliminates an unnecessary program to develop low-enriched naval fuels that would result in a reactor design that is inherently less capable, more expensive, and unlikely to support the significant cost savings associated with life-of-ship submarine reactors.

Enhances Support for Cyber and Energy Security Initiatives. The Budget supports increased funding for cyber and energy security initiatives, recognizing the seriousness of the threat against critical infrastructure, in line with the 2019 Worldwide Threat Assessment of the U.S. Intelligence Community and the National Cyber Strategy. To support broad, interagency cybersecurity efforts, the Budget provides funding in multiple programs, including $185 million for the Office of Cybersecurity, Energy Security, and Emergency Response. This funding would support early-stage R&D activities, in coordination with the energy sector, that improve cybersecurity and resilience throughout the supply chain, protecting critical infrastructure from both natural and man-made events.

Emphasizes American Energy Dominance. The United States has among the most abundant and diverse energy resources in the world, including oil, gas, coal, nuclear, hydro, and renewables. The Budget supports an array of efforts that emphasize and strengthen that unique advantage, leveraging the Nation's position as a global leader in energy production and technological innovation.

> *"[I]nstead of relying on foreign oil and foreign energy, we are now relying on American energy and American workers like never before."*
>
> President Donald J. Trump
> May 14, 2019

The Budget recognizes the emergence of the United States as a top producer of energy in the world, becoming the world's largest oil producer in 2018, transitioning to a net petroleum exporter in late 2019, and projected to become a net petroleum exporter for the 2020 calendar year. As a result, the commercial sector ably produces the energy needed to guard against supply disruptions in the world market. The Budget proposes a slight reduction in Government ownership of petroleum products to fund higher priorities across the energy landscape, including AI and quantum science. The Administration continues to seek strategic opportunities to utilize America's resources and innovative technology to strengthen America's position as a world leader.

The Budget also makes strategic investments to accelerate the development of the next generation of American energy technologies and solutions. This includes $2.8 billion across the Applied Energy Office portfolio to support early-stage R&D and targeted later-stage R&D. This investment helps enable the private sector to develop and deploy the next generation of solutions to usher in a more secure, resilient, affordable, and integrated energy system.

To promote efficiency and maximize impact, the Budget maintains momentum on the Advanced Energy Storage and Harsh Environment Materials Initiatives launched in fiscal year 2020 and establishes a new Critical Minerals Initiative to elevate and coordinate critical minerals activities through a national laboratory-led team modeled after the Grid Modernization Laboratory Consortium.

The Budget also supports extracting critical minerals from coal and coal byproducts as one of many non-thermal, non-power uses of coal. Research into advanced coal processing, and manufacturing of coal-based materials and products would help to develop new markets for coal, ensuring that the world's largest coal reserves would be put to good use in next-generation coal-based products and technologies. Meanwhile, robust investments in carbon capture, utilization, storage, and power generation efficiency would ensure that the existing coal power generation fleet is greener and more efficient than ever before, and ready to serve the Nation for decades to come.

Nuclear energy is also critical to the Nation's energy mix and the Budget supports an array of programs to advance nuclear energy technologies. This portfolio promotes revitalization of the domestic industry and the ability of domestic technologies to compete abroad. The Budget provides $1.2 billion for R&D and other important nuclear energy programs, including nearly $300 million for the construction of the Versatile Test Reactor—a first of its kind fast reactor that would help the private sector develop and demonstrate new technologies.

Supports Nuclear Fuel Cycle Capabilities. On July 12, 2019, the President determined that "...the United States uranium industry faces significant challenges in producing uranium domestically and that this is an issue of national security." The Budget establishes a Uranium Reserve for the United States to provide additional assurances of availability of uranium in the event of a market disruption.

Manages Nuclear Waste. One large hurdle that still faces the nuclear industry is the disposal of spent nuclear fuel. The Administration believes the standstill has gone on too long. The Administration is strongly committed to fulfilling its legal obligations to manage and dispose of the Nation's nuclear waste and will not stand idly by given the stalemate on Yucca Mountain. To create momentum and ensure progress, the Administration is initiating processes to develop alternative solutions and engaging States in developing an actionable path forward. In parallel, the Budget supports the implementation of a robust interim storage program and R&D on alternative technologies for the storage, transportation, and disposal of the Nation's nuclear waste, with a focus on systems deployable where there is a willingness to host.

Maintains a Commitment to Clean Up. The Administration is committed to making progress on cleaning up waste from nuclear weapons production. The Federal Government's environmental and disposal liabilities are $595 billion as of September 30, 2019. DOE is responsible for $505 billion of these liabilities related to nuclear weapons production. The Budget includes $6.1 billion for 16 sites remaining to be cleaned up to meet environmental regulatory requirements.

Aligns Infrastructure Priorities. It is long past time for the Federal Government to divest infrastructure that can be more efficiently maintained by the private sector or local partnerships. The Budget proposes to sell the transmission assets owned and operated by the Power Marketing Administrations (PMAs), including those of the Southwestern Power Administration, Western Area Power Administration, and Bonneville Power Administration. The Budget also proposes to authorize the PMAs to charge rates comparable to those charged by for-profit, investor-owned utilities, rather than being limited to cost-based rates, for electricity. This is a commonsense shift that lessens the burden on the Federal taxpayer. The vast majority of the Nation's electricity needs are met through investor-owned utilities. Reducing or eliminating the Federal Government's role in electricity transmission infrastructure ownership, thereby increasing the private sector's role, and introducing more market-based incentives, including rates, for power sales from Federal dams would encourage a more efficient allocation of economic resources and mitigate risk to taxpayers.

Addresses Unnecessarily Burdensome Energy Efficiency Regulations. Through research and reasonable regulatory actions, DOE will seek opportunities for further improvements in energy efficiency, with an emphasis on solutions that promote consumer choice, the comfort of building occupants, and the performance of labor-saving products, devices, and equipment. Building on the recent light bulb rule success, DOE will pursue improvements to other household appliances through its standards program to improve product efficiency and meet the everyday needs of American households. In addition, DOE will demonstrate the benefits of the revamped Process Rule saving time and money for stakeholders and taxpayers alike through more effective implementation of energy efficiency standards program.

DEPARTMENT OF HEALTH AND HUMAN SERVICES

Funding Highlights:

- The mission of the Department of Health and Human Services (HHS) is to protect and strengthen the health and well-being of Americans by fostering sustained advances in medicine, public health, and social services.

- The Budget continues to support the Administration's commitment to reforming the healthcare system and to reducing prescription drug prices. The Budget also invests in child care to support America's working families and promotes work among able-bodied adults receiving assistance.

- The Budget prevents waste, fraud, and abuse, ensuring sound stewardship of taxpayer dollars. Consistent with the President's Executive Order 13890, "Protecting and Improving Medicare for Our Nation's Seniors," the Budget aligns Medicare payments to providers with seniors' clinical needs and the cost of care rather than the site of care, and also includes other proposals to eliminate wasteful spending, preserve benefits and access to care, and enhance choice and competition.

- The 2021 Budget requests $94.5 billion for HHS, a 10-percent decrease from the 2020 enacted level. The Budget proposes $1.6 trillion in net mandatory health savings, reducing longer-term deficits by eliminating wasteful spending while preserving beneficiaries access to care, enhancing competition, and prioritizing Federal resources for the most vulnerable.

The President's 2021 Budget:

The Budget supports the mission of HHS while creating a streamlined Federal Government that promotes the most efficient and effective use of taxpayer dollars. The Budget invests in: combatting the opioid epidemic; supporting services for serious mental illness; ending the HIV epidemic in America; protecting and improving the Medicare program for seniors; and supporting pro-life principles.

Combats the Drug Abuse and Opioid Epidemic. While real progress has been made in the struggle against the drug abuse and opioid overdose epidemic, too many people are still suffering from opioid addiction; the Centers for Disease Control and Prevention (CDC) reports 67,367 drug overdose deaths in 2018. The Budget invests $5 billion in HHS to combat the opioid epidemic, making critical investments in research, surveillance, prevention, treatment, access to overdose reversal drugs, and recovery support services. This funding includes $1.6 billion, an $85 million increase from the 2020 enacted level, for State Opioid Response grants, which support prevention, treatment, and recovery support services. States are also given flexibility to use these funds to address the emerging drug issue, which is the increasing number of overdoses related to psychostimulants, including methamphetamines.

Helps Americans Suffering from Mental Illness. Americans with serious mental illness (SMI) face significant challenges getting the care they need. In 2018, 47.6 million adults had a mental illness, of whom 11.3 million suffered from SMI, meaning their mental illness substantially interfered with or limited major life activities. More than one out of every three individuals with SMI does not receive mental healthcare and those that receive care encounter a fragmented mental health system that is difficult to navigate. The Budget promotes methods of delivering care that improve outcomes for individuals with SMI. The Budget includes $225 million for Certified Community Behavioral Health Clinics (CCBHC) expansion grants, and extends, through 2021, the CCBHC Medicaid demonstration programs to improve community mental health services for the eight States currently in the demonstration. These activities make it easier for individuals with mental illness and their families to navigate the healthcare system and get services that they need. In addition, the Budget includes $125 million to help schools, community organizations, first responders, and other entities identify mental health issues and help affected youth and other individuals get the treatment they need.

Individuals with SMI are more likely to be homeless and have poorer health status than the general population. The Budget includes an additional $25 million in HHS to expand primary healthcare services for the homeless in cities with high rates of unsheltered homelessness. In addition, some individuals with SMI need hospitalization, yet there are not always enough inpatient beds to serve them. Under current law, Medicaid cannot pay for certain inpatient stays at Institutions for Mental Diseases (IMDs). The Budget modifies the Medicaid IMD exclusion to provide targeted flexibility to States to provide inpatient mental health services to Medicaid beneficiaries with SMI, as part of a comprehensive strategy that includes improvements to community-based treatment.

Continues the Initiative to End the HIV Epidemic in America. The 2021 Budget includes $716 million for the second year of the multiyear initiative to eliminate new HIV infections in America. Each year, there are approximately 40,000 new HIV infections in the United States, the majority clustered in a limited number of counties. The United States has the ability to end the epidemic, with the availability of effective biomedical interventions such as antiretroviral therapy and pre-exposure prophylaxis (PrEP). The Budget includes: $371 million for CDC to reduce new HIV infections; $302 million for Health Resources and Services Administration (HRSA) to deliver HIV care through the Ryan White HIV/AIDS Program and to supply testing, evaluation, prescription of PrEP, and associated medical costs through the Health Centers program; $27 million to the Indian Health Service (IHS) to tackle the epidemic in American Indian and Alaska Native communities; and $16 million for the National Institutes of Health (NIH) for evaluation activities to identify effective interventions to treat and prevent HIV.

Improves Maternal Health in America. Women in the United States have higher rates of maternal mortality and morbidity than in any other developed nation—and the rates are rising. The Budget provides $74 million in new resources to address this significant public health problem by focusing on four strategic goals: 1) achieve healthy outcomes for all women of reproductive age by improving prevention and treatment; 2) achieve healthy pregnancies and births by prioritizing quality improvement; 3) achieve healthy futures by optimizing postpartum health; and 4) improve data and bolster research to inform future interventions.

Supports the President's Health Reform Vision. The Budget includes an allowance for the President's health reform vision. While Americans have the best healthcare options in the world, rising healthcare costs continue to be a top financial concern for many Americans. The President's great healthcare vision will ensure better care at lower costs. Americans deserve affordable, personalized care that puts them in control and provides peace of mind. The President's healthcare reforms will protect the most vulnerable, especially those with pre-existing conditions, and provide the affordability, choice, and control Americans want, and the high-quality care that all Americans deserve.

> "[W]e're creating a healthcare system that protects vulnerable patients, makes healthcare more affordable, gives you more choice and control, and delivers the high-quality care Americans deserve."
>
> President Donald J. Trump
> October 3, 2019

The President's vision would build on efforts outlined in the Executive Order 13877, "Improving Price and Quality Transparency in American Healthcare To Put Patients First," to provide greater transparency of healthcare costs and enshrine the right of a patient to know the cost of care before it is delivered. It focuses on lowering the price of medicine, ending surprise medical bills, breaking down barriers to choice and competition, and reducing unnecessary regulatory burdens. The President's reforms will ensure healthcare is affordable and accessible for all Americans. Reforms will give Americans more control over healthcare choices and improve incentives for cost control. Reforms will also prioritize Federal resources for the most vulnerable and provide assistance for low-income individuals. Medicaid reform will restore balance, flexibility, integrity, and accountability to the State-Federal partnership. Medicaid spending will grow at a more sustainable rate by ending the financial bias that currently favors able-bodied working-age adults over the truly vulnerable.

Ensures Federal Funds Protect Life and Conscience Rights. The Budget prioritizes the value of human life by ensuring that Federal funding does not support abortions. The Budget proposes to prohibit Federal funding, such as in the Title X Family Planning and Medicaid programs, for certain entities that provide abortion services. The Budget also protects conscience rights, prohibits coercion in healthcare, and allows private parties to enforce such rights in Federal court. With these protections, the Administration will continue to ensure robust protection of conscience rights and religious liberty.

Protects and Improves the Medicare Program. The Budget includes proposals to eliminate wasteful spending, preserve beneficiaries' access to care, and enhance choice and competition, consistent with Executive Order 13890. The Budget prioritizes use of the trust funds to pay for seniors' healthcare and incentivizes quality and efficiency in Medicare. The Budget proposes to align payments for post-acute care with patients' needs and the most clinically appropriate site of care, while expanding access to telehealth services. The Budget would extend the solvency of the Medicare program by at least 25 years for America's seniors.

Supports Drug Pricing and Payment Reforms. The 2021 Budget includes an allowance for bipartisan drug pricing proposals. The Administration supports legislative efforts to improve the Medicare Part D benefit by establishing an out-of-pocket maximum, improving incentives to contain costs, and reducing out-of-pocket expenses for seniors. The Administration also supports changes to bring lower-cost generic and biosimilar drugs to patients. These efforts would increase competition, reduce drug prices, and lower out-of-pocket costs for patients at the pharmacy counter.

Addresses Improper Payments in Medicare and Medicaid. In 2019, $1 out of every $15 spent in Medicare, and $1 out of every $7 spent in Medicaid, were considered an improper payment. Improper payments include intentional fraud and abuse, as well as unintentional payment errors, both of which are harmful to the integrity of the Federal Government and to taxpayers. The Budget includes proposals to reduce the monetary loss from improper payments and strengthen the integrity and sustainability of the Medicare program. In addition, the Budget proposes reforms to improve stewardship of taxpayer dollars by strengthening the Centers for Medicare and Medicaid Services' (CMS) ability to address weaknesses in provider screening, enrollment, and identification, as well as beneficiary eligibility determinations in Medicaid. The Budget strengthens CMS's ability to recover overpayments due to incorrect eligibility determinations in the program. Combined with investments in the Health Care Fraud and Abuse Control program, the Budget provides the resources and tools necessary to combat waste, fraud, and abuse and to promote high-quality and efficient healthcare.

Advances American Kidney Health. The Budget includes proposals consistent with the goals outlined in Executive Order 13879, "Advancing American Kidney Health," to transform how kidney disease is prevented, diagnosed, and treated. The Budget would allow individuals with Medicare-covered kidney transplants to retain lifetime coverage for immunosuppressive drugs, and improve oversight of Organ Procurement Organizations, ensuring that deficiencies do not continue unexamined for an extended period of time. The Budget also encourages more living kidney donors by expanding reimbursement for travel and other donation-related costs.

Improves Access to Rural Healthcare. The Budget includes proposals to address the healthcare needs of rural America. The Budget proposes to expand access to telemedicine services by offering increased flexibility to providers who serve predominantly rural or vulnerable patient populations, including IHS providers and providers participating in Medicare payment models requiring financial risk. The Budget proposes to modify payments to Rural Health Clinics to ensure that Medicare beneficiaries continue to benefit from primary care services in their communities. To address the trend of rural hospital closures, the Budget proposes to allow critical access hospitals to voluntarily convert to rural standalone emergency hospitals and remove the requirement to maintain inpatient beds. In addition, the Budget maintains funding for Rural Health Outreach grants in HRSA.

Strengthens IHS. IHS provides comprehensive clinical and public health services to over 2.6 million American Indians and Alaska Natives in 37 States, but the Agency faces longstanding challenges that affect its ability to effectively provide quality healthcare and oversight. The Administration has taken steps to address these challenges, most notably through the formation of a Presidential Task Force on Protecting Native American Children in the IHS System in March 2019. The Budget supports key reforms, including those that bolster recruitment and retention of quality healthcare professionals and expand telehealth to IHS beneficiaries. The Budget maintains dedicated funding to address accreditation challenges at IHS facilities, and continues the multiyear effort to modernize its aging Electronic Health Record system.

Prioritizes Critical Health Research and Supports Innovation. The Budget provides $38 billion for innovative research at NIH to improve public health, $4 billion above the level requested in the 2020 Budget. NIH would continue to address the opioid epidemic and emerging stimulants, make progress on developing a universal flu vaccine, prioritize vector-borne disease research, and support industries of the future. The Budget funds the second year of the Childhood Cancer Data Initiative to further America's understanding of the unique causes of, and the best cures for, childhood cancer.

Advances Vector-Borne Disease Prevention and Control. The threat of mosquito and tick-borne diseases continues to rise in the United States. Cases of tick-borne diseases, such as Lyme disease and Rocky Mountain spotted fever, affected nearly 60,000 Americans in 2017. The Budget includes $66 million for CDC's vector-borne disease activities, a $14 million increase compared to the 2020 enacted level which focuses on tick-borne diseases. The Budget also invests in NIH research to improve the Nation's understanding of vector-borne diseases.

Enhances Influenza Vaccines and Health Security. The Budget supports Executive Order 13887, "Modernizing Influenza Vaccines in the United States to Promote National Security and Public Health," by providing a $95 million increase, compared to the 2020 enacted level, across HHS for influenza vaccine manufacturing infrastructure and innovation; advanced research and development of improved vaccines, therapeutics, and diagnostics; international pandemic preparedness; improved non-egg-based vaccines; and improved vaccine coverage nationwide. The Budget improves access to non-egg-based influenza vaccines for Medicare beneficiaries by proposing a change in Medicare payment for influenza vaccines. The Budget also funds HHS biodefense and emergency preparedness procurement through the BioShield program and the Strategic National Stockpile, and includes $175 million to support CDC's global health security activities, an increase of $50 million compared to the 2020 enacted level.

Reforms Oversight of Tobacco Products. The Budget proposes to move the Center for Tobacco Products out of the Food and Drug Administration (FDA) and create a new agency within HHS to focus on tobacco regulation. This new agency would be led by a Senate-confirmed Director in order to increase direct accountability and more effectively respond to this critical area of public health concern. A new agency with the singular mission on tobacco and its impact on public health would have greater capacity to respond strategically to the growing complexity of new tobacco products. In addition, this reorganization would allow the FDA Commissioner to focus on its traditional mission of ensuring the safety of the Nation's food and medical products supply.

Strengthens Work Requirements to Promote Self-Sufficiency. The Budget improves consistency between work requirements in federally funded public assistance programs, including Medicaid and Temporary Assistance for Needy Families (TANF), by requiring that able-bodied, working-age individuals, aged 18-65 years old, find employment or participate in individualized work activities for a minimum of 20 hours per week, in order to receive welfare benefits, unless they fall into an exempt category or have an individual or geographic hardship. This requirement would enhance service coordination for program participants, improve the financial well-being of those receiving assistance, and ensure federally funded public assistance programs are reserved for the most vulnerable populations.

> *"At the heart of our reforms is democratizing choice and control—by giving it to parents. We are focused on improving the quality of care; expanding affordable options that meet the needs of each family; and removing regulatory barriers that make it difficult to start in-home or faith-based child education services."*
>
> Ivanka Trump
> Advisor to the President
> December 12, 2019

Supports Children and Families in Achieving Their Potential. The Budget proposes a $1 billion one-time investment for States to build the supply of care and stimulate employer investment in child care, and funds child care and early learning to help families access and afford the care they need. The Budget maintains funding for Head Start and the Child Care and Development Block Grant at HHS. The Budget also supports States in serving families and children in the child welfare system by increasing State flexibilities, reducing administrative burdens, and investing in evidence-based resources. In addition, the Budget promotes evidence building and innovation to strengthen America's safety net, proposes improvements to the TANF program, and supports efforts to get noncustodial parents to work. Together, these proposals reflect the Administration's commitment to help low-income families end dependency on government benefits and promote the principle that gainful employment is the best pathway to financial self-sufficiency and family well-being.

Addresses the Humanitarian Needs of Unaccompanied Alien Children. The Budget includes $2.0 billion in discretionary funding and a $2.0 billion mandatory contingency fund to ensure that HHS is able to provide high-quality services to all unaccompanied alien children referred to its care and that HHS has the capacity to manage the inherent uncertainty in this program.

DEPARTMENT OF HOMELAND SECURITY

Funding Highlights:

- The Department of Homeland Security (DHS) safeguards the American people and the homeland by preventing terrorism; securing and managing U.S. borders; administering and enforcing U.S. immigration laws; defending and securing Federal cyberspace; and ensuring disaster resilience, response, and recovery.

- The 2021 Budget prioritizes funding to secure the Nation's borders, including approximately $2 billion to construct additional border wall along the U.S. Southwest border, strengthen and enforce U.S. immigration laws, and respond to and recover from major disasters and large-scale emergencies.

- The Budget proposes to eliminate $535 million in unnecessary Federal spending for Federal Emergency Management Agency (FEMA) grant and training programs that have failed to demonstrate results, supplant State and local government responsibilities, and provide funding to maintain investments that are not Federal responsibilities.

- The 2021 Budget requests $49.7 billion for the Department of Homeland Security, excluding $2.4 billion for the U.S. Secret Service, which the Budget proposes to transfer to the Department of the Treasury. Including the U.S. Secret Service, the Budget request is $52.1 billion, a $1.6 billion or 3.2-percent increase from the 2020 enacted level.

The President's 2021 Budget:

DHS protects Americans from threats by land, sea, air, and cyberspace, on a constant and continuous basis year round. The Department prioritizes smart, innovative, and effective programs to prevent terrorism, promote cybersecurity, secure America's borders, enforce U.S. immigration laws, and lead the Federal Government's coordinated and comprehensive response to major disasters and other large-scale emergencies. The men and women of DHS work tirelessly to ensure the safety, preparedness, and resilience of the Nation. The Budget includes increased funding for border security, immigration enforcement, cybersecurity, disaster recovery, response and preparedness, critical maritime and aviation assets, and front line personnel. The Budget would allow the Department to adapt to new and evolving threats and challenges in order to protect the American people, the homeland, and U.S. economy.

In addition to aggressively pursuing the resources necessary to support border security and immigration control, the Administration is calling upon the Congress to enact immigration reforms, including ending chain migration, ending the visa lottery program, and moving from low-skilled migration to a merit-based immigration system. These needed reforms would increase wages of U.S. workers, shrink the deficit, and raise living standards for both U.S.-born and immigrant workers.

Secures the Borders of the United States. Each day, DHS works to protect the American people and economy by preventing the illegal movement of people and contraband across U.S. borders while facilitating legitimate trade and travel. As depicted in the chart below, the number of people determined to be inadmissible at U.S. ports of entry, or apprehended for illegally crossing the border, grew by over 87 percent from 2018 to 2019, with family units increasing by 227 percent.

Border security remains a top Administration priority, and the Budget continues to implement the President's direction to secure the U.S. Southwest border. Building on prior year investments, the Budget requests $2 billion to construct approximately 82 miles of additional border wall along the U.S. Southwest border. With funding made available from 2017 to 2020, the Administration will build up to approximately 1,000 miles of border wall along the Southwest border. The additional 82 miles of border wall provided in the Budget would provide the U.S. Customs and Border Protection (CBP) with important cross-border impedance and denial capability and contribute to CBP's risk-based plan to secure the entire border.

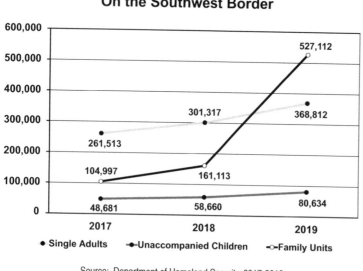

Increased Illegitimate Cross-Border Activity On the Southwest Border

Source: Department of Homeland Security, 2017-2019.

The Budget also: provides $182 million to hire 750 Border Patrol Agents, 300 Border Patrol Processing Coordinators, and support staff; includes $83 million for the 600 CBP Officers funded in 2019; and invests $317 million in non-wall border and trade security investments, including $40 million for a new Humanitarian Care Center. In addition, the Budget includes $1.6 billion to continue to modernize U.S. Coast Guard vessels and aircraft that patrol and provide life-saving rescue missions across the Nation's coastal borders. The Budget includes funding for a second polar icebreaker to ensure America is at the forefront of safeguarding uninterrupted, year round commercial activity, trade, and supply routes and confirming America's leadership role in the Arctic and Antarctic.

Prioritizes Enforcement of Immigration Laws. The Budget provides discretionary and mandatory funding to promote the Administration's immigration and border security priorities and to ensure the safety and security of American communities. While the Budget provides a robust level of immigration and border security activities, these resources alone would not address the need for meaningful immigration reform, which can only be achieved through closing existing loopholes in U.S. immigration laws. The Administration stands ready to work with the Congress to achieve these important reforms.

Funds Additional U.S. Immigration and Customs Enforcement (ICE) Agents. The Budget provides $544 million to hire an additional 4,636 ICE law enforcement officers, immigration court prosecuting attorneys, and additional critical support staff to reach a total of 6,000 staff to carry out this vital national security mission. This additional staff would ensure ICE is able to manage a growing docket of non-detained aliens that: require additional resources to locate and arrest after receiving a final order of removal; or are absconders from the Alternatives to Detention program. In addition, the Budget includes $55 million to support improved personnel recruitment and retention efforts, and facilitate more efficient hiring practices. Funding of $3.1 billion is provided for 60,000 detention beds to ensure ICE has the ability to detain criminal aliens and those ordered removed in absentia, as well as aliens apprehended at the border.

Improves Border and Trade Infrastructure. The Administration proposes the creation of a Border and Trade Security Modernization Fund to provide the additional mandatory funding resources necessary to support the President's border and trade security initiatives and priorities. These resources would be available to fund additional Administration investments for infrastructure, technology, systems, and processes related to trade and travel. The Administration plans to work with the Congress to identify funding and offsets for these activities.

Maintains a Critical Employment Verification System. The employment of illegal aliens by companies is a violation of the law, harms U.S. workers, and contributes to human smuggling, document fraud, identity theft, money laundering, and labor violations. The E-Verify system is an online tool that allows businesses to easily and accurately determine the eligibility of their employees to work in the United States. E-Verify is available at no cost to employers and 98 percent of employees are automatically confirmed as authorized to work either instantly or within 24 hours. The Administration continues to require the use of E-Verify by Federal contractors to ensure the proper utilization of Federal dollars.

Secures U.S. Transportation Systems. The Transportation Security Administration (TSA) secures not just aviation, but also mass transit systems, passenger and freight railways, pipelines, highways, and ports. The Budget supports a pay raise to Transportation Security Officers and supports the deployment of new technologies, including 30 Computed Tomography systems to the Nation's highest risk airports, and other new technologies to increase the effectiveness and efficiency of security operations for all modes of transportation. Approximately $8.2 billion is included in the Budget to support TSA employees and technology that ensures the free movement of people and commerce.

Combats Violence and Terrorism. The Budget provides $80 million across various DHS components for a nationwide, community-based initiative to counter targeted violence and prevent terrorism. DHS will continue to partner with local community stakeholders and organizations that provide support services to de-escalate individuals who may be vulnerable to radicalization before those individuals cross a criminal threshold. Together with the Department of Justice's expansion of the Disruption and Early Engagement Program and in partnerships with the Offices of the U.S. Attorneys, the Federal Bureau of Investigation, local law enforcement, and mental health professionals, the Administration is coordinating efforts to combat targeted violence and prevent terrorism within the homeland.

Invests in Disaster Resilience. The Budget provides investments for the Disaster Relief Fund to ensure communities are prepared for future disasters and to help affected communities that are continuing to recover from past disasters. The Budget also supports reforms to disaster policies that would make disaster response and recovery more effective and less costly for taxpayers.

The Budget proposes a $407 million competitive National Security and Resilience grant program that would be rigorously evaluated to demonstrate how FEMA is supporting communities to make the Nation safer and better prepared. This grant, combined with the Building Resilient Infrastructure and Communities grant program, would help State and local communities build resilience and protect against both man-made and natural hazards. The Budget continues to prioritize funding grant programs where results can be measured, instead of funding formula grants that supplant State and local responsibilities.

Addresses the Cybersecurity Workforce Shortage. The *Delivering Government Solutions in the 21ˢᵗ Century* plan and Executive Order 13870, "America's Cybersecurity Workforce," included several initiatives to solve the Federal cybersecurity workforce shortage by establishing unified cyber workforce capabilities across the civilian enterprise. The Budget includes funding to support DHS's Cyber Talent Management System, which reflects the exemption of DHS's cyber workforce from many of the hiring and compensation requirements and restrictions in existing law under title 5 of the United States Code. The Budget also includes additional funding for the Cybersecurity and Infrastructure Security Agency (CISA) to lead a Government-wide cybersecurity workforce program for all Federal cyber professionals, including an interagency cyber rotational program, a cybersecurity training program for all Federal cyber professionals, and a cyber-reskilling academy. CISA will also spearhead the President's Cup Competition, as described in Executive Order 13870.

Supports Network and Critical Infrastructure Security. The Department continues to play a major role in securing and building cybersecurity resilience for the Nation's most critical infrastructure, including Government networks. In partnership with key stakeholders, DHS identifies and manages the most critical national cybersecurity risks. The Budget includes more than $1.1 billion for DHS's cybersecurity efforts. These resources would increase the number of DHS-led network risk assessments from 1,800 to more than 6,500—including assessments of State and local electoral systems. The Budget also supports additional tools and services, such as the EINSTEIN and the Continuous Diagnostics and Mitigation programs, to reduce the cybersecurity risk to Federal information technology networks.

Strengthens the U.S. Secret Service. The Budget provides $2.4 billion for the U.S. Secret Service, fully supporting the Agency's dual missions of protecting the Nation's leaders while securing America's financial systems. The Budget proposes to transfer the U.S. Secret Service from DHS to the Department of the Treasury. As the Agency transitions to a new department, the Budget supports an additional 119 U.S. Secret Service special agents, officers, and professional staff and continues efforts to rightsize the Agency in order to allow it to perform its important missions. The Budget also proposes investments in protective equipment and technology, consistent with recommendations of independent reviews of U.S. Secret Service operations.

Focuses on Sound Budgeting. The Budget proposes to shift $215 million in Overseas Contingency Operations (OCO) funding for the U.S. Coast Guard into the Department's base budget. This furthers the Administration's goal of ensuring that the OCO request funds only temporary overseas warfighting operations and does not fund enduring operations "off budget."

DEPARTMENT OF HOUSING AND URBAN DEVELOPMENT

Funding Highlights:

- The Department of Housing and Urban Development (HUD) supports safe, decent, and affordable housing for Americans and provides access to homeownership opportunities.

- The Budget reflects the President's commitment to reforming programs to encourage work and self-sufficiency, and provides targeted but fiscally responsible investments that assist vulnerable low-income households.

- The Budget eliminates wasteful programs that have failed to demonstrate effectiveness, such as the Community Development Block Grant (CDBG) and HOME Investment Partnerships Programs (HOME), recognizing that State and local governments are better equipped to respond to local conditions. These eliminations would save taxpayers $4.8 billion in 2021.

- The 2021 Budget requests $47.9 billion in gross discretionary funding for HUD, an $8.6 billion or 15.2-percent decrease from the 2020 enacted level.

- Despite the overall reduction, the Budget maintains rental assistance for all 4.6 million low-income families currently served by HUD.

The President's 2021 Budget:

HUD supports affordable housing for low-income families and provides access to homeownership for traditionally underserved homebuyers. Affordable housing provides families with critical stability that bolsters the economy, strengthens communities, and improves the quality of life for the American people. HUD's Federal Housing Administration (FHA) plays a critical role in helping creditworthy, first-time homebuyers achieve sustainable homeownership. To further these goals, the Budget eliminates programs that have failed to demonstrate effectiveness and strategically invests $47.9 billion to support HUD's core functions, ensuring HUD programs remain a vital resource to the most vulnerable low-income families and first-time homeowners.

The Budget provides $41.3 billion for HUD's rental assistance programs to maintain services to all currently assisted low-income families, while re-proposing reforms in the Administration's Making Affordable Housing Work Act of 2018 and uniform work requirements for work-able households. These legislative reforms would empower families to achieve self-sufficiency and reduce program costs, placing these programs on a more fiscally sustainable path. In addition, the Budget makes a number of targeted investments for low-income families, such as increasing housing options for the elderly and persons with disabilities, removing lead from housing, and protecting against carbon monoxide poisoning. The Budget also provides sufficient funding for homeless assistance grants, as the Administration continues to strengthen efforts to reduce the number of homeless persons living on the streets. To support assisted households to live independently and enhance their quality of life, the Budget also expands key programs that promote self-sufficiency and increase earnings. Further, the Budget prioritizes accountability and efficiency by supporting HUD's multiyear Financial Transformation and information technology modernization efforts.

Eliminates Major Block Grants. The Administration continues to propose eliminating programs that lack measurable outcomes or are ineffective. The Budget eliminates CDBG, a program that has expended more than $150 billion since its inception in 1974, but has not demonstrated sufficient impact. Studies have shown that the allocation formula, which has not been updated since 1978, is ineffective at targeting funds to the areas of greatest need, and many aspects of the program have become outdated.

The Budget also eliminates HOME, which has not been authorized since 1994. State and local governments are better positioned to more comprehensively address the unique market challenges and local policies that lead to affordable housing problems. To support State and local efforts, the White House Council on Eliminating Regulatory Barriers to Affordable Housing is working to identify and support successful practices for removing burdensome rules and regulations that raise the cost of housing development.

Reforms Rental Assistance. The Budget continues providing rental assistance to 4.6 million low-income families. To constrain cost growth, the Budget reproposes rent reforms that would require work-able individuals to shoulder more of their housing costs while providing an incentive to increase their earnings. However, the Budget would mitigate the impact of the proposed reforms on the elderly and persons with disabilities. The proposal would also reduce administrative burden and provide communities with flexibility to adopt alternative rent structures aligned with local needs. The Budget also continues to incorporate uniform work requirements for work-able individuals.

Enhances the Moving to Work Demonstration. The Budget reduces administrative burden and increases transparency for Public Housing Authorities (PHAs) participating in the Moving to Work Demonstration, which provides PHAs with flexibility in designing and testing policies to better serve their residents and communities. As HUD expands the demonstration to additional PHAs, the proposal would facilitate local PHA efforts to better focus on the demonstration's goals of increasing cost-effectiveness, encouraging resident self-sufficiency, and increasing housing choice.

Expands Housing Options for Low-Income Elderly and Persons with Disabilities. The Budget requests $180 million to construct approximately 1,200 new units of housing for the elderly and housing for persons with disabilities. By providing rental assistance and supportive services in settings that prioritize universal design and accessibility, HUD can help residents delay or prevent the need for more institutional settings.

Supports Communities in their Efforts to Reduce Homelessness. The Budget provides $2.8 billion for the Homeless Assistance Grant (HAG) programs to continue supporting approximately 1.1 million individuals who experience homelessness each year. HAG primarily funds the Continuum of Care program, which provides competitive funding to support coordinated and locally driven community-based networks of programs to prevent and address homelessness across the Nation. Within this total, the Budget requests $280 million for Emergency Solutions Grants to support emergency shelter, rapid re-housing, and homelessness prevention. The Administration will also begin a new initiative to reduce unsheltered homelessness. Funding would support comprehensive and coordinated interventions to reduce street homelessness, and would be targeted to select cities that have experienced the largest increases in unsheltered homelessness in recent years.

Promotes Economic Mobility and Improves Quality of Life. Connecting HUD-assisted households to supportive services and employment opportunities helps families reduce their reliance on public assistance and boost their economic productivity. The Budget requests $190 million for self-sufficiency programs, including the Jobs-Plus Initiative. A rigorous evaluation has shown that the Jobs-Plus Initiative produces lasting increases in tenant wages, where residents earned an average of $1,141 more per year than they would have earned without the program. The Budget also includes legislative proposals that would expand eligibility of self-sufficiency programs across HUD rental assistance programs to broaden assistance to households.

Leverages Capital for Housing Improvements. The Budget requests additional resources and statutory authorities to convert more Public Housing units to the Housing Vouchers and Project-Based Rental Assistance (PBRA) funding platforms to help preserve the affordable housing stock. The Budget requests $100 million for the Rental Assistance Demonstration (RAD) program to leverage public and private financing to redevelop approximately 30,000 units of Public Housing for low-income families. Recognizing that Federal, State, and local governments share the responsibility to provide affordable housing, the Budget does not request funding for the Public Housing Capital Fund and eliminates the Choice Neighborhoods grant program, but provides sufficient funding for Public Housing operations and maintenance. These eliminations would save $3 billion in 2021.

> *"RAD provides us the solution to preserve this critically needed housing so it remains permanently affordable for future generations."*
>
> Ben Carson
> Secretary
> October 22, 2019

Reduces Lead and Carbon Monoxide Exposure for Low-Income Children. Lead-based paint in housing presents one of the largest threats to the health, safety, and dreams of America's next generation, with more than 23 million homes having significant lead-based paint hazards. HUD also estimates that 1.5 million HUD-assisted households need carbon monoxide detectors installed in their homes. The Budget requests $425 million to promote healthy homes free of lead, carbon monoxide, and other hazards. Research has shown that lead-based paint hazard control is an efficient and effective form of reducing and preventing exposure, generating high returns on investments due to increased lifetime earnings and reduced medical costs. This funding level also includes resources for enforcement, education, and research activities to further support this goal.

Supports Sustainable Homeownership Opportunities and Protects Taxpayers. The Budget preserves access to sustainable homeownership opportunities for creditworthy borrowers through FHA and Ginnie Mae credit guarantees. FHA provides a crucial source of mortgage financing for first-time homebuyers, who accounted for more than 80-percent of FHA-insured home purchase loans in 2019. Consistent with HUD's *Housing Finance Reform Plan*, the Budget requests $20 million to continue modernizing FHA's outdated single-family information technology systems and includes legislative proposals that would strengthen the viability of reverse mortgages, improve FHA's lender enforcement program, and protect taxpayers.

Strengthens HUD's Financial Management. The Budget includes $15 million for the Department's Financial Transformation initiative, a multiyear effort to continue strengthening HUD's financial reporting, accounting operations, and internal controls. This initiative has demonstrated

"We are committed to improving the lives of all families, especially children, by creating safer and healthier homes. One of HUD's priorities is protecting families from lead-based paint and other health hazards."

Ben Carson
Secretary
September 30, 2019

results by resolving recurring audit issues, aligning accounting policies with Federal standards, and automating manual processes.

Seeks to Reform Federal Disaster Recovery Assistance. The Administration seeks to work with the Congress to comprehensively reform and redesign how the Federal Government supports States, local communities, and disaster survivors after large-scale catastrophic disasters. The current status quo—a convoluted web of programs across 17 departments and agencies—is broken, fiscally unsustainable, and does not result in expedient long-term recovery for communities. A notable example is the HUD CDBG Disaster Recovery program, which continues to be slow, unpredictable, and wasteful. Americans deserve a better system that helps communities recover faster, is less confusing, improves outcomes, and protects taxpayer dollars.

DEPARTMENT OF THE INTERIOR

Funding Highlights:

- The Department of the Interior (DOI) conserves and manages natural resources and cultural heritage for the benefit and enjoyment of the American people, provides scientific and evidence-based information about America's natural resources and hazards, supports safe and responsible development of Federal energy resources, fosters rural prosperity, and honors the Nation's trust responsibilities and special commitments to American Indians, Alaska Natives, and U.S.-affiliated island communities to help them prosper.

- The 2021 Budget request for DOI prioritizes wildland fire risk mitigation, energy development programs, and infrastructure improvements on public lands. The Budget eliminates funding for unnecessary or duplicative programs while reducing funds below the 2020 enacted level for lower priority activities, including land acquisition and various grant programs.

- The Budget proposes to eliminate line-item land acquisition projects funding, saving taxpayers $132 million relative to the 2020 enacted level. Eliminating land acquisition projects funding would allow DOI to focus resources on visitor services and facility repairs in existing national parks, refuges, and public lands, which already encompass nearly 500 million acres.

- The 2021 Budget requests $12.7 billion for DOI, a $2.5 billion or 16-percent decrease from the 2020 enacted level, including changes in mandatory programs.

The President's 2021 Budget:

The Department of the Interior protects and manages the Nation's natural resources and cultural heritage, oversees development of energy and mineral resources on Federal lands and waters, provides scientific and other information about the Nation's natural resources, supervises water infrastructure, honors trust responsibilities to American Indians and Alaska Natives, and fulfills commitments to Insular areas. The 2021 Budget reflects the Administration's strong commitment to promoting economic security and energy dominance by developing domestic energy resources. These efforts invest in America's future and prioritize the safety and security of all Americans by reducing U.S. dependency on foreign nations and increasing America's position as an energy exporter.

Each year, hundreds of millions of Americans pursue recreational opportunities such as fishing, hunting, hiking, and wildlife viewing in U.S. national parks, wildlife refuges, and other public lands. Visitors to public lands spend money locally that supports economic prosperity within these local communities. Also, through the purchases of hunting and fishing licenses and equipment, sportsmen and women have generated billions of dollars that are invested back into wildlife and habitat conservation efforts. To better serve these visitors, the Budget supports expanded public access to lands and waters administered by DOI. The Budget also invests in increased access to encourage sporting enthusiasts, conservationists, veterans, minorities, and other underserved communities that traditionally have low participation in outdoor recreation activities to partake in the great outdoors.

> *"The golden era of American energy is now underway."*
>
> President Donald J. Trump
> May 14, 2019

Strengthens America's Energy Security. The Budget prioritizes funding for DOI programs that support the safe and responsible development of energy on public lands and offshore waters. Federal offshore oil and gas production in the Gulf of Mexico continues to set records, averaging 1.8 million barrels per day in 2018. Onshore, the Administration is working aggressively to implement congressional direction to lease land for oil and gas in the coastal plain of the Arctic National Wildlife Refuge. The Department will continue to make new areas available for all forms of energy development—both onshore and offshore—and will prioritize project permitting consistent with industry demand. The Budget also maintains funding for scientific research and data collection by the U.S. Geological Survey (USGS) to inform responsible energy and mineral development and minimize the environmental impacts of these activities. Combined with administrative reforms to streamline permitting processes, these efforts would provide industry with access to the energy resources America needs, while ensuring that taxpayers receive a fair return from the development of these public resources.

Supports Active Forest Management to Reduce Wildfire Risk. The Administration remains unequivocal about the need to accelerate active forest management on Federal lands. The Budget reflects this critical priority by requesting $228 million for DOI's hazardous fuels mitigation work and $177 million for DOI timber programs. Consistent with the objectives and targets under the President's Executive Order 13855, "Promoting Active Management of America's Forests, Rangelands, and other Federal Lands to Improve Conditions and Reduce Wildfire Risk," to promote active forest management, DOI will utilize the full range of available and appropriate forest management tools, including prescribed burns and mechanical thinning to mitigate fuel loads in order to lessen the risk of fire and maintain air quality. Together, these efforts help ensure that Federal lands are healthy and productive, and that rural communities are more resilient to the destructive impacts of wildfire. The Budget responsibly funds wildfire suppression costs, including cap adjustment resources made available to DOI and the Forest Service for 2021.

Supports Law Enforcement Capacity on Public and Trust Lands. DOI serves as the steward of nearly 500 million acres of public lands and more than 56 million acres of tribal trust lands. The Budget keeps visitors and natural resources safe on the Nation's public lands, and promotes safe tribal communities on trust lands by supporting 191 tribal law enforcement programs and special initiatives to confront the opioid crisis and violence in Indian Country. The Budget supports strong and secure borders, with DOI law enforcement efforts focused on the roughly 12 million acres of DOI lands along the United States-Mexico border. The Budget also invests in the United States Park Police, who safeguard lives and protect America's national treasures. In addition, the Budget invests in U.S. Fish and Wildlife Service (FWS) law enforcement efforts to combat illegal wildlife trafficking, including at the U.S. border and ports of entry, in support of the President's Executive Order 13773, "Enforcing Federal Law with Respect to Transnational Criminal Organizations and Preventing International Trafficking."

Invests in Public Lands Infrastructure Fund. The buildings, trails, roads, water systems, and Bureau of Indian Education (BIE) schools the departments manage are deteriorating, evidenced by a deferred maintenance backlog that exceeds $18 billion. To address this backlog, the Budget proposes a $6.5 billion Public Lands Infrastructure Fund to improve and repair BIE schools as well as facilities in national parks and forests, in wildlife refuges, and on other public lands. The Fund would be supported by the deposit of 50 percent of the proceeds received from Federal offshore and onshore energy leases over the 2021-2025 period, subject to an annual limit of $1.3 billion. These investments would improve some of America's most visited parks and public lands that support a multi-billion dollar outdoor recreation economy.

Preserves National Park Service Assets for Future Generations. The National Park Service (NPS) has a long history of preserving and protecting the natural and cultural sites that tell America's story. To continue this tradition and ensure preservation of national parks for generations to come, the Budget provides $314 million to help address NPS's deferred maintenance backlog. Along with the mandatory funding provided by the Public Lands Infrastructure Fund, this funding would help NPS maintain and preserve America's highest priority assets.

Prioritizes Land Management Operations of the NPS, FWS, and Bureau of Land Management (BLM). To protect and conserve America's public lands, the Budget provides $5 billion for land management operations. These resources would ensure access to recreational activities such as hunting, fishing, and camping, and provide safe experiences for visitors. The Budget also advances efforts to streamline operations and reduce unnecessary spending, and proposes substantial resources to address the unsustainable growth rate and associated outyear costs of wild horse and burro herds on Federal lands.

Invests in Essential Science Programs. The Budget invests in USGS science related to natural hazards; water, energy, minerals, and other natural resources; and the health of America's ecosystems and environment. The Budget supports development of the Landsat 9 ground system, as well as research and data collection to inform sustainable energy and mineral development, responsible resource management, and natural hazard risk reduction.

Supports Tribal Sovereignty and Self-Determination. In recognition of its trust responsibilities to American Indians and Alaska Natives, the Budget continues to prioritize funding for core operations that foster tribal sovereignty, sustain tribal governments, and support the effective stewardship of trust resources. The Budget provides $2.9 billion to support programs serving Indian Country, including social services, public safety, infrastructure maintenance and natural resource management. The Budget also supports the BIE's efforts to foster the success of the approximately 46,000 students it serves, and the Bureau of Indian Affairs' (BIA) efforts to address violence in Indian Country, including the disproportionately high numbers of missing and murdered American Indians and Alaska Natives.

Streamlines Reviews and Permitting. DOI is responsible for administering foundational environmental and historic preservation laws nationwide and for managing more than 20 percent of the Nation's lands, which affects the American public and many private stakeholders. The Budget supports DOI in fulfilling these important permitting and review responsibilities in a timely and thorough manner. As an example, the Budget maintains core funding for FWS to conduct Endangered Species Act of 1973 (ESA) consultations, which help facilitate development of infrastructure projects while ensuring threatened and endangered species receive the protections intended by the ESA. The Budget also maintains the BLM's ability to efficiently facilitate and administer development of energy transmission projects.

Eliminates Unnecessary, Lower Priority, or Duplicative Programs. The Budget includes elimination of discretionary Abandoned Mine Land economic development grants that overlap with existing mandatory reclamation grants and National Heritage Areas that are more appropriately funded locally. The Budget also eliminates the Indian Guaranteed Loan Program funding that largely duplicates other existing loan programs serving Indian Country, and National Wildlife Refuge Fund payments to local governments that fail to take into account the economic benefits that refuges provide to neighboring communities. The Budget also proposes to eliminate components of the BIA's Welfare Assistance Program, a supplementary program that largely duplicates other Federal and State programs that serve Indian Country.

> *"Last year,...[Bureau of Indian Affairs, Office of Justice Services] officers successfully stopped thousands of pounds of deadly narcotics from reaching our tribal communities. I applaud the multi-department effort that has led to these drug seizures as it supports the Trump Administration's commitment to protecting its citizens and getting these drugs off the streets."*
>
> David Bernhardt
> Secretary
> June 24, 2019

Reduces Funding for Land Acquisition. The Budget continues to focus on using resources to manage existing lands and assets managed by DOI. The Budget provides $23 million (including balance cancellations) to handle ongoing projects, along with small projects to provide or expand access to hunting, fishing, and outdoor recreation. This proposed level is significantly lower than the 2020 enacted level and would allow DOI to focus resources on supporting activities in existing national parks, refuges, and public lands, which encompass nearly 500 million acres.

Invests in Water Resources and Infrastructure. The Budget invests in the safe, reliable, and efficient management of water resources throughout the United States. The Budget requests $1.1 billion for the Bureau of Reclamation, with an emphasis on operating, maintaining, and rehabilitating existing water resources infrastructure throughout the western United States. Through the Bureau of Reclamation and BIA, the Budget requests a total of $156 million in discretionary funding to implement enacted Indian water rights settlements in support of Federal trust responsibilities to Tribes. The Budget also invests a total of $200 million at the USGS and the Bureau of Reclamation for science to sustain and enhance ground and surface water quality and quantity, and to develop new technologies to respond to the water resources challenges facing the Nation.

DEPARTMENT OF JUSTICE

Funding Highlights:

- The Department of Justice (DOJ) defends the interests of the United States and protects all Americans as the chief enforcer of Federal laws.

- The Budget prioritizes and protects investments in core Federal Government functions such as national security, cybersecurity, violent crime and targeted violence reduction, immigration, drug enforcement, and the opioid epidemic.

- The Budget eliminates wasteful spending, including $505 million reserved for the construction of a new prison that is unneeded due to the declining prison population, significantly delayed due to the site selected, and very costly to taxpayers; and $244 million in annual funding for the elimination of the State Criminal Alien Assistance Program, which is poorly targeted and an ineffective tool to support immigration enforcement.

- The 2021 Budget requests $31.7 billion for DOJ, a $730 million or 2.3-percent decrease from the 2020 enacted level. The Budget targets funding increases to support public safety and national security while reducing or eliminating lower priority spending.

The President's 2021 Budget:

DOJ enforces the laws and defends the interests of the United States; ensures public safety against foreign and domestic threats; provides Federal leadership in preventing and controlling crime; seeks just punishment for those guilty of crimes; and ensures the fair and impartial administration of justice for all Americans. For the second year in a row, the estimated number of violent crimes in the Nation decreased by 3.3 percent in 2018 when compared to 2017. The Department is committed to building on this success by expanding efforts to dismantle criminal networks, disrupt and prosecute human trafficking rings, halt the flow of illegal drugs, support criminal justice reform, and restore law and order to communities. The 2021 Budget requests a total of $31.7 billion to expand the capacity of key law enforcement agencies and strengthen the Department's ability to address the most pressing public safety needs.

Supports Federal Law Enforcement and Strengthens National Security. DOJ is committed to restoring law and order by providing Federal resources where they are most needed and most effective. The Budget provides $16 billion for Federal law enforcement, including the Federal Bureau of Investigation (FBI), the Drug Enforcement Administration (DEA), the United States

Marshals Service (USMS), the Bureau of Alcohol, Tobacco, Firearms and Explosives (ATF), and the Organized Crime and Drug Enforcement Task Forces. These resources support the Department's ability to respond to national security crises, including cybersecurity, counterintelligence, and transnational organized crime. Funding also supports investigations of violent and drug-related crime, and apprehension and prosecution of offenders.

The Budget also transfers the entirety of the ATF alcohol and tobacco regulatory and enforcement responsibilities to the Alcohol and Tobacco Tax and Trade Bureau (TTB) in the Department of the Treasury. This transfer would enable the ATF to hone its focus on activities that protect U.S. communities from violent criminals and criminal organizations, while consolidating duplicative alcohol and tobacco enforcement mechanisms within the TTB. In addition, the operating capability of the DEA's Special Investigative Unit program would retain its critical role in enhancing the Federal Government's ability to pursue threat networks to their source, as prioritized in the National Security Strategy.

Combats Targeted Violence and Addresses Violent Crime. The Administration is committed to furnishing law enforcement and the communities they serve with the tools to effectively protect against targeted violence incidents and respond appropriately in the event of tragedy. The Budget provides $639 million for the Department to surge law enforcement to address violent crime and targeted violence. Of this, $329 million is provided to support additional agents and personnel at DOJ's law enforcement components, and $310 million is devoted to DOJ grant programs supporting State and local law enforcement, including $150 million for STOP School Violence programs, $33 million for Mental Health Collaboration, and $13 million for active shooter trainings.

Enforces Immigration Laws. The Administration remains committed to robust enforcement of the Nation's immigration laws, and ensuring a safe homeland for all Americans. The Budget provides $883 million to support 100 immigration judge teams and to expand DOJ's Executive Office for Immigration Review (EOIR) electronic case management systems. Administration policies have increased immigration enforcement, driving a growing case backlog at EOIR. By the end of 2019, there were more than 987,000 cases pending before the courts, after receiving nearly 444,000 cases during the year, the highest level of initial cases received in EOIR's history. EOIR continues to attack the backlog by bolstering levels of Immigration Judge teams, who are responsible for adjudicating the cases, and through gaining other efficiencies, including modernization of EOIR's information technology systems. The Budget also provides $2.1 billion to support USMS' Federal Prisoner Detention, which is projected to increase in population due to enhanced enforcement of gun, drug, and immigration crimes.

Combatting Human Trafficking

"My Administration is committed to leveraging every resource we have to confront this threat, to support the victims and survivors, and to hold traffickers accountable for their heinous crimes."

President Donald J. Trump
October 11, 2018

Counters Human Trafficking. The Administration is committed to ending the scourge of human trafficking in the United States. The Budget provides $70 million to support the investigative and prosecutorial capacity of the Department, including $44 million for FBI investigations of child sex trafficking, $14 million for U.S. Attorneys prosecution efforts, $6 million for the Criminal Division's Child Exploitation and Obscenity Section, $5 million for the Human Trafficking Prosecution Unit, and $1 million for USMS activities to recover missing children. An additional $123 million is provided to DOJ grant programs supporting State and local efforts to address human trafficking, including $80 million to support victims of trafficking, $40 million to support multi-disciplinary efforts to investigate and prosecute trafficking, and $3 million for human trafficking research.

Promotes Criminal Justice Reform. In addition to prosecuting crime and enforcing the Nation's laws, the Administration proposes to promote public safety by helping prevent individuals who have reentered society from returning to prison. Approximately 95 percent of incarcerated persons will eventually leave prison. However, individuals released from State prison have a five-year recidivism rate of 77 percent, and those released from Federal prison have a five-year recidivism rate of 42 percent. The Administration is committed to breaking this cycle of recidivism by better preparing individuals to reenter communities and mitigating the collateral consequences of incarceration.

> ### Bipartisan Prison Reform
>
> *"Americans from across the political spectrum can unite around prison reform legislation that will reduce crime while giving our fellow citizens a chance at redemption."*
>
> President Donald J. Trump
> November 14, 2018

To meet this challenge, the Budget provides $319 million in new funding for the Bureau of Prisons (BOP) to support robust implementation of the historic FIRST STEP Act of 2018. Of this amount, the Budget provides $244 million to increase residential reentry center capacity by 8,700 beds; $37 million to make medication-assisted drug treatment available at all eligible BOP facilities; $23 million to meet the increasing demand for mental health, life skills, special needs, and educational and vocational programs; and $15 million to bolster other implementation activities. This investment would expand inmate access to evidence-based, recidivism-reducing programs and incentivize participation by allowing inmates to earn earlier transfers to residential reentry centers. In addition, through State and local assistance programs, the Budget provides $88 million for the Second Chance Act grant program to reduce recidivism and help returning citizens lead productive lives.

Tackles the Opioid Epidemic. Today, the United States faces the deadliest drug overdose crisis in American history. More than 67,000 Americans lost their lives to drug overdoses in 2018. Evidence shows that fentanyl, heroin, and prescription opioids are responsible for nearly 47,000 of these tragic deaths. The Department recognizes its critical role in combating prescription opioid misuse and illicit heroin and fentanyl use. The Budget provides $2.4 billion in discretionary resources for the DEA, including an additional $67 million to enhance efforts to identify, investigate, disrupt, and dismantle major drug trafficking organizations and online illicit drug marketplaces impacting the safety and security of communities across the Nation. The Budget also provides $460 million in fee-funded resources for DEA's Diversion Control Fee account to combat the diversion of licit prescription drugs and precursor chemicals for manufacturing illicit synthetic drugs.

These efforts are bolstered by an additional $6 million to support 10 new attorneys and support staff to ensure that the U.S. Attorney's Office will continue to generate drug cases for prosecution. In addition, the Budget includes $361 million for opioid-related State and local assistance including: $160 million for the Comprehensive Opioid Abuse Program to support treatment and recovery, diversion, and alternatives to incarceration programs; $132 million for Drug Courts, Mental Health Courts, and Veterans Treatment Courts; $30 million for Residential Substance Abuse Treatment; $30 million for Prescription Drug Monitoring Programs; and $9 million for Opioid-Affected Youth.

> ### Protecting Americans from Opioids
>
> *"It is time to liberate our communities from this scourge of drug addiction...We can be the generation that ends the opioid epidemic."*
>
> President Donald J. Trump
> October 26, 2017

Supports State and Local Law Enforcement. While the Administration recognizes that both the role and responsibility for funding policing is inherently local, the Budget provides funding for key State and local assistance programs in order to help address the most pressing criminal justice issues impacting America's communities, including $412 million for the Byrne Justice Assistance Grants Program, which provides State and local governments with crucial Federal funding to prevent and control crime. Included in that amount, the Budget provides $40 million for the Project Safe Neighborhoods program, which leverages Federal, State, and local partnerships to address gang violence and gun crime. An additional $97 million is provided for programs supporting research and innovation for law enforcement, including $44 million for the National Institute of Justice, $43 million for the Bureau of Justice Statistics, and $10 million for Paul Coverdell Forensic Science Improvement Grants. The Budget further reflects the Administration's commitment to support rural communities by providing $56 million to grant programs specifically targeted to those communities.

DEPARTMENT OF LABOR

Funding Highlights:

- The Department of Labor (DOL) ensures that American workers, job seekers, and retirees are equipped to succeed in the workforce and ever-changing economy.

- The Budget focuses DOL on its highest priority functions and restores fiscal discipline by eliminating programs that are duplicative, unnecessary, unproven, or ineffective. The Budget also takes steps to reorganize and modernize DOL's operations so taxpayer dollars are spent efficiently.

- The Budget eliminates duplicative and unproven job training programs, saving more than $500 million in taxpayer dollars.

- The 2021 Budget requests $11.1 billion for DOL, a $1.3 billion or 10.5-percent decrease from the 2020 enacted level, including the program integrity cap adjustment.

The President's 2021 Budget:

DOL supports American workers, job seekers, and retirees by providing resources and opportunities to improve their skills, find work, and enter or return to the workforce. The Department also safeguards their working conditions, health and retirement benefits, and wages. The economy is strong, and the unemployment rate is at its lowest recorded level in over 50 years. Workers are the backbone of the strong American economy, and the Nation needs a skilled and productive workforce to keep the economy growing. The Budget puts American workers and taxpayers first by eliminating duplicative, wasteful, and non-essential job training programs and instead investing in evidence-based approaches, such as apprenticeship, to help workers build their skills and remain competitive in the dynamic 21st Century workforce.

Builds a Highly Skilled and Competitive Workforce

Expands Access to Apprenticeship. The Budget invests $200 million in apprenticeship, a proven solution for employers looking for a skilled workforce and workers looking for an affordable path to a secure future. As part of implementing the President's Executive Order 13801, "Expanding Apprenticeships in America," the Department is establishing a new industry-recognized apprenticeship system to modernize and expand the Nation's approach to apprenticeships. Since the start of the Administration, businesses have begun training 626,134 new apprentices. DOL is working to further expand apprenticeships by empowering third-party Standards Recognition Entities to recognize new, industry-driven apprenticeship programs, focusing on those in high-growth sectors where apprenticeships are underutilized, such as healthcare, information technology, and advanced manufacturing.

> *"We live in an age of acceleration, and the skills required for today's jobs are changing more rapidly with each passing year. America needs to adapt its approach to skills education and be more nimble and responsive to the pace of change across all industries."*
>
> Ivanka Trump
> Advisor to the President
> June 24, 2019

Reforms Job Corps. Job Corps is among the most expensive Federal training programs on a per-capita basis and is in need of reform. To that end, the Budget takes aggressive steps to improve Job Corps for the youth it serves by improving center safety, focusing the program on older youth, and closing centers that inadequately prepare students for jobs. In order to create a more effective, streamlined program, the Budget proposes new legislative flexibilities that would enable DOL to more expediently close low-performing centers, target the program to youth who are more likely to benefit from it, and make the necessary capital investments to ensure successful pilot programs. These reforms would save money and improve results by eliminating ineffective centers and finding better ways to educate and provide skill instruction to youth.

Combats Waste, Fraud, and Abuse in the Unemployment Insurance Program. The Federal-State Unemployment Insurance (UI) program has continually had one of the highest rates of improper payments in the Federal Government. More than 10 percent of the program's payments, representing $2.8 billion, are paid to individuals who do not meet the program's eligibility requirements. The Budget takes strong steps to address this problem by providing grants to States to combat the top two root causes of improper payments and emphasize work in their programs, getting claimants off of benefits and back on the job more quickly. The Budget also reduces waste, fraud, and abuse in the UI program with a package of program integrity proposals. These proposals require States to use the tools already at their disposal and allow States to spend certain UI program funds on activities that reduce waste, fraud, and abuse. The Budget also supports the UI Integrity Center of Excellence, which is developing a data hub to allow States to access a fraud analytics database to identify fraud as effectively as possible.

Supports America's Veterans. The Budget supports the transition of the Nation's veterans, servicemembers, and their spouses from active duty to civilian life. The Budget provides funding to better support wounded warriors in the Transition Assistance Program and provides enhanced reemployment services to Gold Star spouses who are seeking to enter the workforce.

Closes the Skills Gap by Training American Workers. The Budget proposes to double the American Competitiveness and Workforce Improvement Act of 1998 fee for the H-1B visa program to prepare American workers for jobs that are currently being filled by foreign workers, especially in science, technology, engineering, and mathematics fields. The increased revenue would support DOL's grants to expand apprenticeship and other high-growth training opportunities and provide additional support for technical-skills instruction at the K-12 and community-college levels through the Department of Education's Career and Technical Education formula grants.

Moves toward Reorganizing and Consolidating the Nation's Workforce Development Programs. The Federal Government has more than 40 workforce development programs spread across 15 Agencies with a total annual cost of approximately $19 billion. The Administration has proposed to streamline the system with a Government-wide restructuring and consolidation proposal and looks forward to working with the Congress to enact it. The Budget takes steps in this direction by eliminating programs that are ineffective, unproven, or duplicative. As part of this long-overdue reorganization of workforce programs, the Budget also transfers the Social Security Administration's Ticket to Work program to DOL, where it would be simplified, streamlined, and improved to better accomplish its goal of getting individuals with disabilities back into the labor force.

> "Every day, we are lifting our forgotten Americans off the sidelines, out of the margins, and back into the workforce."
>
> President Donald J. Trump
> July 19, 2018

Improves the Delivery of America's Economic Statistics. The Budget recognizes the importance of economic statistics to businesses and everyday citizens as they make informed decisions and confidently invest in America's future. The Budget proposes investments in the Bureau of Labor Statistics (BLS) to better understand job-market changes in States and local areas and to improve poverty measurement, including the development of a consumption-based poverty measure. The Budget also continues to support moving the BLS to the Suitland Federal Center, which would save more than $300 million over the lifetime of the new lease.

Supports American Workers and their Families

Supports United States-Mexico-Canada Agreement (USMCA) Enforcement. The historic USMCA agreement will create a more level playing field for American workers, including improved rules of origin for automobiles, which will support better jobs for workers and more business for U.S. manufacturers. The Budget funds implementation and enforcement of the USMCA labor chapter, which includes some of the strongest labor provisions of any U.S. free-trade agreement.

Makes Health Insurance More Affordable for Small Businesses. In Executive Order 13813, "Promoting Healthcare Choice and Competition Across the United States," the President directed the Secretary of Labor to consider expanding access to affordable health coverage for small businesses. The Budget continues to support this initiative by increasing funding for the Employee Benefits Security Administration to develop policy, regulations, and enforcement capacity to enable more employers to adopt the Multiple Employer Welfare Arrangement model and expand access to health insurance for American workers in ways that better fit the modern American workplace.

Rebuilds DOL's Role in Overseeing Union Integrity. To help safeguard labor-union democracy and financial integrity, the Budget takes steps to restore the Office of Labor-Management Standards' investigative workforce, which has fallen by more than 30 percent in the past 10 years. The Budget would strengthen protections for union members by supporting more audits and investigations to uncover flawed officer elections, fraud, and embezzlement.

Protects Americans' Pensions. The Pension Benefit Guaranty Corporation's (PBGC) multiemployer program, which insures the pension benefits of 10 million workers, is at risk of insolvency by 2025. As an important step to protect the pensions of these hardworking Americans, the Budget proposes to add new premiums to the multiemployer program, raising approximately $26 billion in premiums over the next 10 years. At this level of premium receipts, the program is projected to remain solvent over the next 20 years, helping to ensure that there is a safety net available to workers and retirees whose multiemployer plans fail. The Administration looks forward to working with the Congress on bipartisan, comprehensive reform to resolve the multiemployer crisis.

Reforms the Federal Employees' Compensation Act. The Budget proposes to reform the Federal Employees' Compensation Act program, which provides workers' compensation benefits to Federal employees and their survivors. These reforms would save taxpayer dollars by modernizing program administration, simplifying benefit rates, and adding controls to prevent waste, fraud, and abuse.

Puts American Workers First. DOL administers the labor-certification component of foreign temporary work visa programs, which ensure that American workers are not unfairly displaced or disadvantaged by foreign workers. The certification programs lack a reliable workload-based source of funding, which has created recurring seasonal backlogs for employers. The Budget proposes to establish fees to create a workload-based funding source and place responsibility for funding this work on the program's users rather than taxpayers.

Provides for Paid Leave for New Parents. The Budget invests in a better future for Americans with a proposal to provide paid leave to new mothers and fathers, including adoptive parents, so all families can afford to take time to recover from childbirth and bond with a new child. The proposal would allow States to establish paid parental leave programs in a way that is most appropriate for their workforce and economy. The Federal Government is leading by example. At the end of 2019, the Administration secured paid parental leave for the Federal workforce. The Administration looks forward to continuing to work with the Congress to advance policies that would make paid parental leave a reality for families across the Nation.

> *"I am...proud to be the first President to include in my budget a plan for nationwide paid family leave, so that every new parent has the chance to bond with their newborn child."*
>
> President Donald J. Trump
> February 5, 2019

Makes Government More Efficient

Tackles Duplication and Inefficiency at DOL. Many of DOL's administrative activities, including information technology, procurement, human resources, financial management, and physical security are separated across its subcomponents. DOL is centralizing these activities to eliminate duplication, achieve economies of scale, and save money. For example, the Department has avoided over $10 million in unnecessary spending by centralizing its laptop purchasing for DOL employees. DOL will also save money by changing the way it procures goods and services across the Department. By centralizing its procurement functions, DOL will be able to concentrate its contracting expertise, achieve economies of scale, and make better purchasing decisions.

DEPARTMENT OF STATE AND OTHER INTERNATIONAL PROGRAMS

Funding Highlights:

- The Department of State, the U.S. Agency for International Development (USAID), and other international programs promote and advance the national security and economic prosperity of the United States through diplomacy, enhanced security, and fair economic competition.

- The Budget for U.S. international programs advances the Nation's strategic objectives outlined in the 2017 National Security Strategy. The Budget supports new tools to allow the United States to focus on great power competition and respond flexibly to international challenges. The Budget also prioritizes organizational reforms to increase agency effectiveness, prioritize the efficient use of taxpayer dollars, and increase burden-sharing.

- Across the international affairs budget, eliminations of various programs and accounts would save nearly $170 million compared to the 2020 enacted level. These savings include the elimination of earmarked funding to non-Federal and non-profit entities such as The Asia Foundation, which sustains outside fundraising and should rely on private donations and competitive grants rather than taxpayer dollars. Further savings come from reductions to embassy-based small grants for non-strategic events and programs, which have included: $4,800 to send American artists to a poetry festival in Finland; $7,500 for a foreign student to attend Space Camp; and $10,000 to support the Muppet Retrospectacle in New Zealand.

- The 2021 Budget requests $40.8 billion for the Department of State and USAID, an $11.7 billion or 22-percent decrease from the 2020 enacted level. The Budget also requests $1.6 billion for Department of Treasury international programs, a $0.1 billion or 8-percent decrease from the 2020 enacted level.

The President's 2021 Budget:

The 2021 Budget provides the necessary resources for the United States to maintain and expand U.S. influence while safeguarding U.S. economic interests. As great power competition becomes more prevalent, the United States must confront new challenges and meet new realities. To achieve this effectively, the Budget invests in new capabilities to defend American interests and values across the security, trade, and information domains.

The Budget supports America's allies, proposes new avenues to deepen existing relationships, and contains a new approach toward countries that have taken unfair advantage of U.S. generosity. The Budget increases fiscal restraint by eliminating ineffective programs and continuing to support wide-reaching agency reforms. This includes recalibrating American contributions to international organizations; asking other nations to pay their fair share, while maintaining American leadership.

Prioritizes Great Power Competition

Ensures the Indo-Pacific Region Remains Free, Open, Independent, and Counters Chinese Propaganda. The future of the Indo-Pacific, which contains roughly half the world's population and many of the fastest-growing economies, is critical to U.S. security and long-term economic interests. The Budget provides $1.5 billion for the Indo-Pacific, reflecting a strong Administration commitment to ensuring that the region remains free, open, and independent of malign Chinese influence. This funding supports democracy programs, strengthens security cooperation, improves economic governance, and facilitates private sector-led economic growth. A total of $30 million is included in the Budget for the Global Engagement Center dedicated to countering foreign state and non-state propaganda and disinformation from China.

Counters Russian Influence by Strengthening U.S. Allies. The Budget provides $0.7 billion for assistance to Europe, Eurasia, and Central Asia to advance shared security; safeguard the territorial integrity of U.S. allies; support partner countries' efforts to transition away from Russian military equipment; and address weaknesses in the macro-economic environment that the government of Russia seeks to exploit, such as dependence on energy and trade. The Budget also provides $24 million for the Global Engagement Center to counter Russian propaganda and disinformation.

Levels the Playing Field for U.S. Exporters. The Budget promotes the President's trade agenda by providing robust support for the Office of the U.S. Trade Representative (USTR). The Administration is advancing fair and reciprocal trade through agreements with Mexico and Canada, South Korea, Japan, and China, and through ongoing negotiations with the United Kingdom, China, and European countries. These agreements are opening new markets for American exports and creating jobs while protecting American intellectual property. The Budget also supports the Administration's efforts to enforce trade agreements and protect American businesses and workers from trade violations and predatory business practices.

Expands the International Development Finance Corporation (DFC) for Private Sector Development Internationally. The Budget provides $0.8 billion for the DFC to support private-sector growth in less developed countries and to provide a transparent, high-quality alternative to predatory Chinese international lending in the Indo-Pacific and other strategic regions. The Budget allows the DFC to make equity investments, increasing its ability to invest in critical private sector projects. Using these tools, the DFC would complement and enhance U.S. strategic and foreign policy objectives in the developing world.

Expands Defense Financing for America's Allies. The Budget proposes an expanded set of Foreign Military Financing (FMF) loan and loan guarantee programs for NATO and Major Non-NATO Allies to complement traditional FMF grant assistance. With these tools, the United States would increase opportunities for allies to build their militaries around U.S. innovation and quality and transition away from inferior equipment from foreign adversaries. This would increase burden sharing, while bolstering security and improving interoperability, and support the U.S. defense industrial base.

Bolsters Core Diplomatic Efforts

Supports America's Strongest Allies in the Middle East. The Budget fully supports the U.S.-Israel Memorandum of Understanding and includes $3.3 billion in FMF grant assistance to bolster Israel's capacity to defend itself against threats in the region and maintain its qualitative military edge. The Budget also fully supports the U.S.-Jordan Memorandum of Understanding at $1.3 billion and the U.S. diplomatic and security partnership with Egypt, including $1.3 billion in FMF grant assistance.

Empowers Women to Contribute to Global Economic Growth and Political Stability. The Budget promotes women's economic empowerment in developing countries by doubling support for the Women's Global Development and Prosperity (W-GDP) Fund to $200 million. The W-GDP Initiative helps women advance in the workplace, succeed as entrepreneurs, and fully and freely participate in the economy. Despite making up half of the world's population, women remain one of the greatest underutilized resources for growing economies. W-GDP applies rigorous metrics to track and assess progress as the initiative works to economically empower 50 million women across the developing world by 2025. The Budget also supports the meaningful participation of women in conflict prevention, resolution, and recovery as an evidence-based solution for promoting lasting peace and stability through the implementation of the Women, Peace, and Security Act.

> "We resolve that the future of the Western Hemisphere will not be written by socialists and tyrants, but by liberty-loving patriots. Our great destiny is to become the first fully free hemisphere in human history."
>
> President Donald J. Trump
> September 25, 2019

Promotes American Interests Abroad. The Budget requests $4.8 billion for Diplomatic Programs supporting the Department of State's core function of achieving U.S. foreign policy objectives and advancing American interests via 276 embassies, consulates, and diplomatic missions around the world. This funding level sustains and invests in the State Department's workforce, while putting taxpayers first by promoting more efficient operations. The Budget would enable the Department to continue modernizing its Information Technology platform to allow its workforce to do their jobs efficiently, effectively, and securely. In addition, the Budget includes $4.1 billion for consular and border security programs. This critical component of U.S. border security protects the American people while facilitating legitimate travel. The Budget also requests $1.3 billion for USAID Operating Expenses to support USAID personnel in 87 missions.

Prioritizes Embassy Security. The Budget requests $5.4 billion to protect overseas personnel and facilities, including the Department's share of the $2.2 billion requested Government-wide, for new, secure embassy construction, as recommended by the Benghazi Accountability Review Board. This security funding supports the protection of every U.S. diplomatic mission and the thousands of employees who promote U.S. interests and values overseas in dangerous and challenging security environments. In fact, through 2019, with sustained embassy security funding, the Department successfully moved more than 41,000 personnel into safer overseas facilities. The Budget also includes $100 million to bolster maintenance of these facilities. With the proposed level of funding, the Department of State would continue to protect American personnel representing more than 30 agencies, as well as provide services to Americans overseas, in a safe and secure environment.

Improves Stewardship of Taxpayer Dollars and Maintains U.S. Global Leadership

Focuses on U.S. Interests and Promotes Fairer Burden Sharing. The Budget supports the aims of the United States to compete and lead in multilateral organizations, thereby protecting American interests and principles around the world. To do so efficiently and effectively, this is accomplished by fully funding international organizations critical to U.S. national security, and reducing or eliminating funding to other organizations and programs whose results are either unclear or do not directly affect U.S. national security interests. The Budget also continues America's commitment to reevaluate the design and implementation of peacekeeping missions and increase accountability and transparency in all international organizations. In addition, the United States will continue to insist that financial burden sharing be more fair and equitable to the United States and its taxpayers, including through negotiating lower assessment rates and proposing more appropriate contribution levels in the Budget. One recent achievement to advance this objective was the reduction in the assessment rate for NATO, so that the United States is now in line with other major members.

Demands Necessary Reforms at the Multilateral Development Banks (MDBs) while Maintaining U.S. Leadership. The Budget requests $1.5 billion in funding for the MDBs, including support for new pledges to the World Bank's International Development Association and the African Development Fund. The Administration continues to demand reforms that would better align the MDBs with U.S. development and foreign policy goals. Recently negotiated reforms will improve financial management and debt sustainability while increasing the MDB's focus on infrastructure, women's economic empowerment, and assistance to fragile states, when implemented.

Reforms U.S. Humanitarian Assistance while Expecting Others to Do More. The Budget continues the U.S. commitment to assist globally in the event of humanitarian crises, at a more targeted funding level. The Administration remains committed to fundamental restructuring needed to most effectively address evolving conflict-driven crises and best meet the needs of those affected, including helping refugees remain close to their homes until they can safely return. This restructuring is critical to delivering optimal results both for affected populations and for American taxpayers, and is supported by several independent analyses. USAID's new Bureau for Humanitarian Assistance consolidates multiple organizations into a single office to streamline administration of all overseas humanitarian assistance through a new flexible account that can respond to evolving needs. These changes build on USAID's and the State Department's strengths, leveraging USAID's expertise on effective program implementation and State's overall authority over foreign policy, diplomacy, and refugee policy. Under the restructuring proposal, the State Department would maintain its existing staff and continue to run U.S. refugee admissions via a separate account, with transfers from International Humanitarian Assistance account if resettlement needs increase.

Streamlines Foreign Assistance and Concentrates Resources on the Highest Impact Programs. The Budget again proposes to streamline economic and development assistance by eliminating accounts with similar authorities and reducing the request for the consolidated account by 21 percent compared to the 2020 enacted level. This account restructuring would improve flexibility and enable a more balanced consideration of how these programs support prosperity and economic opportunities, and advance American interests and values around the world. In particular, the Budget:

- Re-aligns economic and development assistance to programs with proven impact for the benefit of the American people. This includes efforts to counter Russia, China, and other adversaries; graduate developing countries from foreign aid through self-reliance; and increase trade and investment opportunities.

- Protects investments in economic growth and trade facilitation including funding for Prosper Africa and focuses limited resources on African countries with greater potential to increase two-way trade and investment. This would increase opportunities for American businesses consistent with the President's Africa Strategy.

- Includes the necessary funds to implement the comprehensive set of reforms outlined in the Administration's *Delivering Government Solutions in the 21st Century* plan, including a major structural reorganization of USAID to strengthen core capabilities, increase efficiency, and reduce costs.

Protects Freedom Worldwide. The Budget advances freedom worldwide for all people by supporting programs that counter trafficking in persons and support the freedom of religious and ethnic minorities. The Budget provides $150 million to support persecuted religious and ethnic minorities around the world and promote religious freedom, as well as $60 million to end modern slavery abroad and provide resources for survivors. In order to accomplish these goals, the Budget supports programs that strengthen the rule of law, combats transnational criminal operations, and partners with local and faith-based organizations worldwide. The United States will continue to challenge state and non-state entities that seek to infringe upon the fundamental right of living according to one's own principles.

> *"America stands with believers in every country who ask only for the freedom to live according to the faith that is within their own hearts."*
>
> President Donald J. Trump
> September 23, 2019

Sustains U.S. Leadership in Fighting the HIV/AIDS Epidemic. The Budget provides $658 million for the Global Fund to Fight AIDS, Tuberculosis and Malaria and offers to match $1 for every $3 contributed by other donors. Coupled with appropriated funds, this request would keep the United States on track to meet the Administration's $3.3 billion pledge for the Global Fund's sixth replenishment by 2022. The Budget also requests $3.2 billion for the U.S. President's Emergency Plan for AIDS Relief (PEPFAR), $170 million less than the 2020 Budget. With these resources and 2020 appropriations, PEPFAR would continue to provide lifesaving treatment in over 50 countries, maintain all current patients on treatment, and help recipient countries achieve HIV epidemic control. With these resources, the United States would continue to be the top HIV/AIDS donor in the world.

Protects the United States and the World from Infectious Disease Through the Global Health Security Agenda (GHSA). The Budget sustains the U.S. international partnership with GHSA to defend the Nation from infectious disease outbreaks by building the capacity of countries to prevent, detect, and respond to these threats. The Budget also requests $290 million for Gavi, the Vaccine Alliance, as part of a four year, $1.2 billion pledge for Gavi's upcoming replenishment cycle beginning in 2021. Immunization programs avert an estimated annual 2 to 3 million child deaths globally and are one of the most cost-effective health interventions. The Budget requests $2.2 billion for lifesaving programs addressing nutrition, neglected tropical diseases, tuberculosis, family planning, and maternal and child health. The Budget focuses increased resources on the President's Malaria Initiative, with an emphasis on combatting drug-resistant malarial strains at time when there are over 200 million new cases of malaria per year.

DEPARTMENT OF TRANSPORTATION

Funding Highlights:

- The mission of the Department of Transportation (DOT) is to ensure that the Nation has the safest, most efficient, and modern transportation system in the world. The Department also ensures the system improves the quality of life for all American people and communities, from rural to urban, and increases the productivity and competitiveness of American workers and businesses.

- The Budget proposes a historic 10-year, $810 billion reauthorization of surface transportation programs, including highway, transit, rail, highway safety, and hazardous materials safety programs, including important reforms to provide critical investments in the Nation's transportation infrastructure. The Budget includes an additional $190 billion for additional infrastructure investments, across a range of sectors, for a total of $1 trillion in infrastructure investment.

- The Budget eliminates a required set-aside for the Transportation Alternatives program that restricts States from choosing the most meritorious projects. This elimination provides additional flexibility to use the resources within the Surface Transportation Block Grant Program to support projects that rehabilitate or expand highways in a manner that supports interstate or regional commerce.

- The Budget requests $21.6 billion in discretionary budget authority for 2021, a $3.2 billion or 13-percent decrease from the 2020 enacted level. The Budget also provides $66.2 billion in mandatory contract authority and obligation limitations, a $5 billion or 8-percent increase from the 2020 enacted level.

The President's 2021 Budget:

DOT is responsible for supporting and enabling a high functioning transportation system—to move both people and goods safely and efficiently in order to support jobs and economic growth. The Budget supports necessary investments that ensure the Nation's air, surface, and maritime transportation systems are safe.

The Budget proposes a 10-year reauthorization of surface transportation programs, including $755 billion in mandatory spending from the Highway Trust Fund, and $55 billion in authorizations of discretionary budget authority from the General Fund. Combined with the Administration's separate proposal on investing an additional $190 billion in infrastructure across multiple sectors, including transportation, the Budget provides $1 trillion in direct Federal investment in infrastructure.

New Initiative to Help Rural Communities Access DOT Financial Assistance

As part of its commitment to ensuring that all communities can access and compete for DOT financial assistance, the Administration announced the Rural Opportunities to Use Transportation for Economic Success (ROUTES) Initiative. Under this initiative, the Build America Bureau and other modes will offer rural stakeholders additional resources and support to identify and apply for DOT financial assistance. The initiative was created with the recognition that rural communities have important infrastructure needs (e.g., a disproportionate amount of highway fatalities occur in rural areas), but often lack the capacity to develop competitive applications for DOT financial assistance. The ROUTES Initiative builds on other DOT initiatives to address the unique needs of rural areas, such as the Transportation Infrastructure Finance and Innovation Act loan program's rural project initiative and the Railroad Rehabilitation and Improvement Financing Express loan program initiative.

Invests in America's Surface Transportation Infrastructure. The FAST Act authorized contract authority and discretionary budget authority for highway, transit, rail, and hazardous material programs through 2020. The Budget proposes to reauthorize all modes included in the FAST Act, but also streamline and consolidate accounts and programs to improve efficiencies and program effectiveness. The Budget also proposes to end the recent practice of appropriating additional discretionary budget authority for the highway and transit formula programs, and instead reflect that funding through higher contract authority levels provided from the Highway Trust Fund. In total, the Budget proposes an 8-percent increase in 2021 for highway and transit formula programs from the level provided in the last year of the FAST Act. The Budget also provides for a 3.8-percent increase to the National Highway Traffic Safety Administration (NHTSA) and the Federal Motor Carrier Safety Administration (FMCSA) from the level provided in the last year of the FAST Act.

Reauthorizes Highway Programs. The Budget provides $50.7 billion in 2021 and $602 billion over the 10-year reauthorization period for Federal Highway Administration (FHWA) programs. The proposal would provide States and other stakeholders the resources and certainty to build a strong, modern, and world-class highway infrastructure network that advances the Nation's safety, economy, mobility, and global competitiveness. The proposal responds to input from FHWA's partners and stakeholders, by continuing to expand program and funding flexibilities for States, and removing red tape and other barriers to innovation and efficiency. The proposal also maintains safety as the number one focus. These reforms are guided by the recognition that States and localities, not the Federal Government, are best equipped to understand the infrastructure challenges and investments needs of their communities.

Reauthorizes Transit Programs. The Budget provides $13 billion in 2021 and $155 billion over the 10-year reauthorization period for Federal Transit Administration programs, to support mobility and accessibility for American workers and improve their communities. The proposal would streamline grant programs to improve flexibility and reduce administrative burdens and would focus on maintaining current transit assets to improve the state of good repair of the Nation's transit systems. The proposal would also bolster transit systems' safety, support underserved areas, and leverage opportunities to utilize new and emerging technologies.

Reauthorizes Highway Safety Programs. The Budget provides a combined $1.7 billion in 2021 and $19.8 billion over the 10-year reauthorization period for NHTSA and FMCSA programs, to continue the Department's efforts to save lives, prevent injuries, and reduce economic costs incurred from traffic accidents involving both passenger and commercial motor vehicles. In 2021 NHTSA and FMCSA will begin conducting a crash causation study, the first such study in more than 15 years. The Budget also builds on the existing work of the Department to reduce regulatory burdens while improving safety and promoting innovation with emerging technologies such as automated driving systems.

Supports Competitive Grant Programs. The Budget continues to invest in competitive grant programs that partner with communities to deliver surface transportation projects with significant benefits. The Budget provides $1 billion to the Better Utilizing Investments to Leverage Development (BUILD) program. The Administration proposes to authorize the BUILD program for the first time in its surface transportation proposal. The Budget also provides $1 billion in discretionary resources to the Infrastructure for Rebuilding America program. These programs use competitive processes to target resources efficiently and effectively, and DOT will focus on strengthening these processes in 2020.

Improves Aviation Safety. The Budget requests $14.2 billion for the Federal Aviation Administration (FAA), including $37 million for targeted investments that would improve the FAA's ability to respond to industry innovation, safety, and accountability. This includes $30 million to improve aviation oversight, following recommendations from the Boeing 737 MAX investigations and reviews, and to make investments in the systems that support the FAA's ongoing safety oversight.

Reforms Amtrak to Provide Better Services. Amtrak's network has not been significantly modified since Amtrak's inception 50 years ago, and long distance routes continually underperform, suffering from low ridership and large operating losses of roughly half a billion dollars annually. Simply put, Amtrak trains inadequately serve many rural markets while not serving many growing metropolitan areas at all. The Administration believes that restructuring the Amtrak system can result in better service at a lower cost, by focusing trains on better-performing routes, while providing robust intercity bus service connections. To accomplish this transformation, the Budget provides $550 million in transitional grants for States and Amtrak to begin the process to restructure the network. In addition, the Budget provides $936 million in direct grants to Amtrak, to support investment on the Northeast Corridor and existing State-supported lines, and to assist Amtrak in this transition.

Provides Reforms to the Essential Air Service Program (EAS). Originally designed as a temporary program over 40 years ago, EAS subsidizes commercial air service to rural airports. EAS costs have more than doubled in the past 10 years and many EAS flights are left unfilled and have high per passenger subsidy costs. In addition, several EAS-eligible communities are relatively close to major airports. There are more efficient ways to target Federal funds to address the transportation needs of rural communities. The Budget proposes to reduce the discretionary funding for EAS and reform the program to target Federal funds for communities most in need of their services. The Budget would continue the mandatory resources for EAS at approximately $154 million.

Advancing Use of Unmanned Aircraft Systems into the National Airspace

FAA is working to safely integrate unmanned aircraft systems (UAS) into the national airspace. The UAS Integration Pilot Program (IPP) is a unique project that brings together diverse stakeholders to further safe integration and address community engagement, including concerns of State, local, and tribal governments. The IPP brings State, local, and tribal governments together with private sector entities, such as UAS operators or manufacturers, to test and evaluate the integration of civil and public drone operations into the national airspace. There are nine IPPs, which began in 2018, and have resulted in new drone operations such as night operations, flights over people and beyond the pilot's line of sight, package delivery, and development and testing of new technologies for detect-and-avoid capabilities and data security. The FAA also recently proposed new regulations that require remote identification of UAS in the national airspace, to address safety, national security, and law enforcement concerns and enable greater operational capabilities.

DEPARTMENT OF THE TREASURY

Funding Highlights:

- The Department of the Treasury (Treasury) manages the U.S. Government's finances, promotes conditions that enable stable economic growth, protects the integrity of the financial system, and combats financial crimes and terrorist financing.

- The Budget proposes strategic reforms and investments to streamline Treasury's operations, bolster Treasury's national security and law enforcement capacity, enhance the taxpayer experience, and lower the deficit.

- The Budget eliminates $248 million in unnecessary spending related to Community Development Financial Institutions (CDFI) Fund awards that are no longer needed given the maturity of the CDFI industry.

- The Budget requests $15.7 billion in base discretionary resources for Treasury's domestic programs, including $2.4 billion for the U.S. Secret Service, which the Budget proposes to transfer from the Department of Homeland Security. Excluding the request for the U.S. Secret Service, the Budget request is $13.3 billion or $291 million and 2.2-percent above the 2020 enacted level.

The President's 2021 Budget:

The 2021 Budget would modernize and strengthen Treasury's ability to efficiently manage the Nation's economy, protect U.S. financial systems from criminal and national security threats, and serve as the fiscal steward of the Federal Government. The Budget proposes targeted investments to disrupt terrorist financing, hold rogue states and human rights abusers accountable, and detect and deter financial crimes. The Budget also supports Treasury's role as chair of the Committee on Foreign Investment in the United States (CFIUS) to address current and future national security risks. In addition, the Budget enhances the Department's functions as the Federal Government's revenue collector, financial manager, and economic policymaker. By putting taxpayers first, demonstrating fiscal restraint, and eliminating wasteful and unnecessary spending, the Budget builds on recent economic progress, spurs innovation, and helps create the economy of tomorrow.

Returns the U.S. Secret Service to Treasury. The U.S. Secret Service was established in 1865 within Treasury to combat then-widespread counterfeiting of U.S. currency, and remains the sole office charged with the protection of U.S. currency. The Homeland Security Act of 2002 transferred the U.S. Secret Service and 21 other Federal agencies into the newly created Department of Homeland Security to better protect the Nation from terrorism and other threats to U.S. safety and security.

Technological advancements in recent decades, such as cryptocurrencies and the increasing interconnectedness of the international financial marketplace, have resulted in more complex criminal organizations and revealed stronger links between financial and electronic crimes and the financing of terrorists and rogue state actors. The Budget proposes legislation to return the U.S. Secret Service to Treasury to create new efficiencies in the investigation of these crimes and prepare the Nation to face the threats of tomorrow.

Invests in Economic Security. Treasury's Office of Terrorism and Financial Intelligence (TFI) combats terrorists, rogue regimes, proliferators of weapons of mass destruction, human rights abusers, and other illicit actors by denying their access to the financial system, disrupting their revenue streams, and degrading their ability to cause harm. TFI plays an increasingly important role in countering the Nation's most critical national security and illicit finance threats, thereby reducing long-term risk, instability, and potential economic losses. The Budget requests $173 million for TFI, a 40-percent increase relative to 2017 funding levels, to strengthen TFI's data analytics, intelligence, sanctions, and enforcement capabilities.

Bolsters the Prevention, Detection, and Investigation of Financial Crimes. The Financial Crimes Enforcement Network (FinCEN) links law enforcement and intelligence agencies with financial institutions and regulators, leading to the discovery and prosecution of money-laundering schemes and other crimes that cause lasting harm to Americans and the economy. The Budget requests $127 million for FinCEN to prevent and address financing of terrorism, money laundering, and other crimes. These resources would enhance FinCEN's protection of data collected under the Bank Secrecy Act, which would increase its value to law enforcement agencies, and expand its efforts to combat emerging virtual currency and cybercrime threats.

Strengthens Review of Foreign Investment. CFIUS determines national security risks from certain foreign investment. In 2018, CFIUS was expanded and strengthened by the Foreign Investment Risk Review Modernization Act of 2018 (FIRRMA). FIRRMA updates CFIUS to better address national security concerns, including by broadening the authorities of the President and CFIUS regarding national security concerns arising from certain foreign non-controlling investments and real estate transactions that previously fell outside CFIUS's jurisdiction. The Budget requests $35 million for Treasury to continue the swift implementation of FIRRMA.

Improves Tax Administration and Modernizes Taxpayer Systems. Filing taxes is the most significant interaction that many Americans have with the Federal Government each year. The Internal Revenue Service (IRS) collects approximately $3.6 trillion in tax revenue annually and processes more than 255 million tax returns and forms resulting in more than $300 billion in tax refunds. The Budget proposes $12.0 billion in base funding to modernize the taxpayer experience and ensure that the IRS can fulfill its core tax filing season responsibilities. The Budget provides $300 million to continue IRS efforts to modernize its information technology (IT) infrastructure and enhance taxpayers' ability to interact with the IRS securely and electronically, improving the time it takes for IRS to resolve concerns.

Bankrupting Terrorists and Rogue Regimes

TFI works around the clock to collect and analyze intelligence and effectively deploy its arsenal of sanctions and other financial enforcement tools against criminals and national security threats. In the past two years alone, TFI has cut off the flow of billions of dollars to Iran, disrupted networks that provided the brutal Syrian regime with access to oil and financing, and expanded sanctions to punish Russian aggression and corrupt Kremlin-linked oligarchs. The Budget continues the Administration's investment in economic tools to advance foreign policy and address emerging threats, such as the use of cryptocurrencies in money laundering and terrorist financing.

For example, the Budget includes funding to digitize more IRS communications to taxpayers so they can respond quickly and accurately to IRS questions; create a call-back function for certain IRS telephone lines so taxpayers do not need to wait on hold to speak with an IRS representative; and make it easier for taxpayers to make and schedule payments online. In developing these tools, the IRS conducts surveys and interviews with taxpayers to understand what taxpayers want and then tests the new tools with taxpayers so that they are easy to use.

The Budget also proposes legislation enabling additional funding for new and continuing investments to expand and strengthen tax enforcement. These additional proposed investments are estimated to generate approximately $79 billion in additional revenue at a cost of $15 billion, yielding a net savings of $64 billion over 10 years.

The Budget also includes several proposals to ensure that taxpayers comply with their obligations and that tax refunds are only paid to those who are eligible, including: improving oversight of paid tax preparers; giving IRS the authority to correct more errors on tax returns before refunds are issued; requiring a valid Social Security Number for work in order to claim certain tax credits; and increasing wage and information reporting.

Manages the Nation's Finances More Effectively. The Bureau of the Fiscal Service (BFS) manages the Nation's debt and is the Federal Government's primary accounting and financial service provider. In 2019, BFS issued approximately $11.7 trillion in marketable Treasury securities, processed the collection of more than $4.26 trillion in Federal receipts, and distributed more than $3.7 trillion in payments. The Budget provides funding to enhance the cybersecurity of the IT systems that support these activities and touch the lives of every American taxpayer. The Budget also empowers everyday Americans who have invested in their Nation by funding an online tool that would allow individuals to verify ownership of unredeemed savings bonds dated after 1974.

Connects Communities with Development Capital while Protecting Taxpayers. The Budget proposes to end funding for the CDFI Fund discretionary grant and direct loan programs. More than two decades ago, the CDFI Fund was created to jumpstart an industry at a time when CDFIs had limited access to private capital. The CDFI industry now has ready access to the capital needed to extend credit and offer financial services to underserved communities, eliminating the need for Federal grants. The Budget also proposes to eliminate the Bond Guarantee Program requirement for a relending account, which adds unnecessary cost and complexity to the program.

Brings Accountability and Transparency to Treasury's Regulatory Oversight Functions. Consistent with recommendations made in Treasury's June 2017 report to the President on banks and credit unions, the Budget proposes that the Congress establish funding levels for the Office of Financial Research (OFR) and the Financial Stability Oversight Council (FSOC) through annual appropriations bills. OFR and FSOC, established by the Dodd-Frank Wall Street Reform and Consumer Protection Act, are currently able to set their own budgets, which circumvents congressional approval and oversight. OFR has taken administrative steps to further the goals in the Treasury report, including an organizational realignment to significantly reduce staffing and operating expenses to better focus OFR on its core mission to support FSOC and the financial regulatory community.

Modernizes and Streamlines Oversight of Alcohol and Tobacco Industries. The Budget provides resources to enable the Alcohol and Tobacco Tax and Trade Bureau (TTB) to continue modernizing its tax and IT systems to better serve its customer base and the public. The Budget also proposes to transfer all alcohol and tobacco responsibilities from the Department of Justice's (DOJ's) Bureau of Alcohol, Tobacco, Firearms and Explosives (ATF) to TTB, which has extensive expertise relating to the alcohol and tobacco industries. By allowing ATF to focus exclusively on its firearms and explosives mandates, this transfer would enable Treasury and DOJ to more efficiently and effectively protect the Nation.

DEPARTMENT OF VETERANS AFFAIRS

Funding Highlights:

- The Department of Veterans Affairs (VA) is committed to providing military veterans and their survivors with the benefits, care, and support they have earned through sacrifice and service to the Nation.

- The 2021 Budget continues to fulfill the President's promise to veterans by making critical investments in high priority initiatives that ensure veterans receive top quality care, benefits, and services—wherever they work or live. The Budget supports key Administration priorities such as veteran suicide prevention and opioid abuse prevention programs, and continues to integrate the changes enshrined in the VA MISSION Act of 2018, providing veterans greater choice in and access to the medical care they deserve. The Budget also supports other critical priorities, such as electronic health record modernization and information technology (IT) enhancements, to strengthen efficiency, transparency, and accountability within the Department.

- The 2021 Budget eliminates waste and enhances efficiency by accelerating the planned deployment for a modern medical care scheduling system. VA tested a modern scheduling system in Columbus, Ohio, which demonstrated: a more than 50 percent productivity improvement in scheduling staff; a 38-percent reduction in case manager overtime, resulting in a potential savings of $9.9 million per year for VA when fully deployed; an expansion of same day appointment availability; and an increase in new and established patient appointments by five and six percent, respectively. VA will expand these benefits to more veterans in multiple medical centers in 2021 and to all veterans nationwide by 2025.

- The Budget requests $105.0 billion for VA, a $12.9 billion, or 14.0-percent increase from the 2020 enacted level, including changes in mandatory programs. In addition, the Budget requests $94.2 billion in advance appropriations for VA medical care programs in 2022 to ensure the Department has sufficient resources to continue providing the quality medical services veterans have earned.

The President's 2021 Budget:

VA's mission is to deliver benefits, care, and support to America's military veterans and their families; the Department also continues to implement reforms to improve care and benefits. The Budget provides the necessary resources to meet the Nation's commitment to veterans to help them recover from illnesses, injuries, or wounds sustained due to their military service and to enable their successful reintegration into civilian life.

President Trump Is Committed to Supporting Every Brave American Who Has Served Our Nation

"We must strive to build communities that truly serve, support, and protect our veterans from the very first moment they return to civilian life."

President Donald J. Trump
August 21, 2019

The Budget fully funds the operation of veterans healthcare, one of the largest integrated healthcare systems in the United States with over 9.2 million enrolled veterans, provides disability compensation benefits to nearly 5.7 million veterans and their survivors, and administers pension benefits for approximately 393,000 veterans and their survivors.

In addition, the Budget invests in a broad range of veteran services and programs, including: educational assistance for nearly one million students; rehabilitation and employment benefits for approximately 131,000 veterans; servicemember and veteran group life insurance plans for approximately six million enrollees; more than three million active home mortgage loans; and memorial and burial benefits in more than 156 national cemeteries and thousands of other cemeteries across the Nation.

Champions VA Programmatic Initiatives

Prioritizes Veterans Affairs Medical Care Funding. The Budget provides $90.0 billion, a 12.7-percent increase above the 2020 enacted level, including funding to continue the integration of the expanded VA MISSION Act of 2018 requirements, providing greater choice for many veterans regarding their healthcare decisions. The Budget also includes $1.2 billion for the expansion of the Caregivers program, which provides stipend payments to eligible veterans.

Invests in Veteran Suicide Prevention. The Budget also provides $313 million, a 32-percent increase over the 2020 enacted level, to support the Administration's veteran suicide prevention initiatives, including the National Roadmap to Empower Veterans and End Suicide, a population-based, public health model encouraging partnerships at the national, regional, and local levels. These efforts support evidence-based approaches for suicide prevention that intersect with various sectors, including State and local governments, faith communities, employers, schools, and healthcare organizations.

Funds Opioid Abuse Prevention Programs. The Budget provides $504 million for opioid prevention and treatment, a 19-percent increase over the 2020 enacted level. This amount includes $121 million for comprehensive programs for addiction treatment and recovery that expand and integrate implementation of evidence-based programs related to opioid and pain care for veterans. Funding supports expansion of multidisciplinary efforts, including: providing naloxone kits to at-risk VA patients and VA first responders; addressing staffing and resource deficiencies at pain management teams and pain clinics; expanding VA's use of predictive analytics to target veterans at-risk for overdose events; supporting recommendations from the President's Commission on Combating Drug Addiction and the Opioid Crisis; and establishing a "tele-hub" to provide opioid pain, addiction prevention, and treatment using telehealth capabilities.

Provides Funding for VA's Electronic Health Record Modernization. The Budget also provides $2.6 billion, an 82-percent increase over the 2020 enacted level, to support a unified electronic health record (EHR) between the Department of Defense (DOD) and VA. The funding enables VA to double the number of sites that transition to the new EHR in 2021, consistent with DOD, and accelerates a new scheduling system throughout the VA enterprise five years sooner than originally planned. This planned acceleration would enable VA to increase provider productivity and veteran access to care.

Modernizes VA IT and Infrastructure. The Budget provides $4.9 billion, a 12.4-percent increase over the 2020 enacted level, to fund critical investments in IT modernization, infrastructure, and customer service to enhance the veteran experience. Specifically, this funding enables the Department to enhance mission critical IT systems supporting VA MISSION Act of 2018 implementation, facilitating Blue Water Navy claims processing, enhancing supply chain management, and implementing financial management business transformation.

> **President Trump Is Working Tirelessly to Provide the Benefits and Services that Our Brave Veterans Deserve**
>
> *"My administration is committed to taking care of every warrior that returns home as a veteran."*
>
> President Donald J. Trump
> August 21, 2019

Blue Water Navy Claims Processing. The Budget also provides $137 million for VA to support Blue Water Navy claims processing, enabling the hire of new claims processors to augment staffing capacity and complete scanning requirements not finished during 2020.

Increases Access to Burial and Memorial Benefits. The Budget includes $360 million, a 9.4-percent increase over the 2020 enacted level, to expand veteran access to memorial benefits, deliver premier services to veterans' families, and provide perpetual care for more than four million gravesites. The Budget also supports expanding and sustaining 156 cemeteries, which include 11 cemeteries transferred from the Department of the Army as part of the *Delivering Government Solutions in the 21st Century* plan, and 33 soldiers' lots and monument sites.

Promotes Efficiency, Transparency, and Accountability

Targets Investments to Create Efficiencies. The Budget prioritizes investments in areas that create future savings and that improve the efficiency and effectiveness of VA programs. Targeted investments in IT systems, including more than $310 million for cloud migration and aging infrastructure replacement to support the new EHR system, would result in cost savings as VA consolidates data centers and reallocates resources to higher priority needs. VA is also committed to modernizing its disability compensation program and identifying innovative pilot programs aimed at providing opportunities for disabled veterans seeking employment.

Streamlines Government. The Budget also promotes fiscal discipline by better aligning a unified EHR between DOD and VA. This would give doctors instant and seamless access to veterans' full-service health records and history and enable faster, smarter connections between military and veteran health information. VA will also continue to change the way it buys medicine and equipment by tapping into DOD's centralized acquisition system.

Reduces Waste, Fraud, and Abuse. The Budget fully funds the Offices of Enterprise Integration and Accountability and Whistleblower Protection to ensure VA programs improve oversight, accountability, and performance within the Department. The Budget also provides $228 million, an $18 million increase above the 2020 enacted level, for the Office of the Inspector General to strengthen accountability, promote transparency, and reduce waste, fraud, and abuse.

CORPS OF ENGINEERS—CIVIL WORKS

Funding Highlights:

- The Army Corps of Engineers civil works program (Corps) develops, manages, restores, and protects water resources primarily through the construction, operation and maintenance, and study of water-related infrastructure projects. The Corps is also responsible for regulating the development of navigable waters of the United States and works with other Federal agencies to help communities respond to, and recover from floods and other natural disasters.

- The Budget focuses Federal investment where it is most warranted within the three primary mission areas of the Corps to address the most significant risks to public safety or to provide a high economic or environmental return to the Nation. The Budget also targets accelerating the completion of ongoing projects. The Budget continues to propose reforms to how the Nation invests in water resources projects, by enabling greater local participation in Corps projects.

- The Budget eliminates funding for projects that are better suited to be carried out by States and local communities. The Budget proposes the Corps implement more robust tools and greater transparency to control spending and ensure taxpayer funding isn't being utilized for unnecessary or wasteful projects. The Administration encourages the Congress to join it in supporting the approval of projects based on merit and need.

- The 2021 Budget requests $6 billion for the Corps, a $1.7 billion or 22-percent decrease from the 2020 enacted level.

The President's 2021 Budget:

The Corps has three main missions: flood and storm damage reduction; commercial navigation; and aquatic ecosystem restoration. The Corps also regulates development in navigable waters and wetlands. While the Agency has had a significant impact on water resources development throughout its history, current approaches to funding, constructing, and maintaining projects often do not deliver benefits in either a timely or cost-effective manner. The current paradigm for investing in water resources development is not optimal; it can deter rather than enable States, local communities, and the private sector from making important investments on their own, even when they are the primary beneficiaries. The Budget lays the foundation for accelerating the construction of infrastructure and increasing competition in the delivery of projects, thereby resulting in faster completion of projects and cost savings. The Budget focuses Federal resources where they are most warranted, encourages more non-Federal leadership, and removes barriers that can impede the ability of non-Federal parties to move forward on their own with investments in water resources infrastructure they deem priorities.

Prepares for the Future Not the Past

Accelerates Completion of Ongoing Construction Projects. The Budget keeps the Federal Government's promise to complete ongoing construction projects that provide a high economic or environmental return to the Nation or address a significant risk to public safety more quickly and more cost effectively. By proposing not to start any new construction projects, the Budget enables the Corps to focus on completing these ongoing priority projects faster and at a reduced cost, allowing the affected communities to see their benefits sooner. The Budget also recognizes the need to change the way future construction investments are funded, with less reliance on Federal appropriations. For example, the Budget provides $250 million for innovative partnerships between the Federal Government and non-Federal sponsors to accelerate completion of projects.

Prioritizes Operating and Maintaining Existing Infrastructure. The Budget gives priority to operating and maintaining existing water resources infrastructure and improving its reliability. Maintenance of the key features of this infrastructure is funded; this includes navigation channels that serve the Nation's largest coastal ports and the inland waterways with the most commercial use, such as the Mississippi and Ohio Rivers and the Illinois Waterway.

Reaffirms the President's Commitment to Restoring the Everglades

"Congress needs to help us complete the world's largest intergovernmental watershed restoration project ASAP! Good for Florida and good for the environment."

President Donald J. Trump
May 13, 2019

The Budget includes $250 million for the South Florida Ecosystem Restoration Program.

Increases Flexibility to Respond to Future Natural Disasters. The Budget provides $50 million in the Flood Control and Coastal Emergencies Account, and $50 million in the Harbor Maintenance Trust Fund for urgent emergency response work following flood-related major disaster declarations, pursuant to the Robert T. Stafford Disaster Relief and Emergency Assistance Act.

Empowers States and Local Communities to Accelerate Water Resources Projects. The Budget expands the Corps' use of section 1043 of the Water Resources Reform and Development Act of 2014, as amended, by including $250 million for an innovative program under which the Corps would transfer appropriated funds to non-Federal sponsors that decide to construct a project on their own. Non-Federal implementation of projects, where appropriate, would accelerate the construction of more infrastructure projects and create efficiencies in their delivery. Under this program, the Corps would issue a solicitation for proposals from non-Federal sponsors to construct their own projects using a combination of Federal and non-Federal funding. Other projects specifically funded in the Budget may also qualify for implementation under section 1043. The Budget also proposes to extend section 1043, which expired in 2019.

Prioritizes Core Functions

Improves the Transportation of Goods on the Nation's Inland Waterways. The Budget proposes to reform the laws governing the Inland Waterways Trust Fund, including an annual per-vessel fee for commercial users; to help finance future capital investments on these waterways and a portion of the cost of their operation and maintenance. The current diesel fuel tax is insufficient to support the users' share of these costs.

Divests the Washington Aqueduct. The Budget proposes to sell the Washington Aqueduct, the wholesale supply system for Washington D.C.; Arlington County, Virginia; the City of Falls Church, Virginia; and parts of Fairfax County, Virginia. The Corps owns and operates the Aqueduct, which is the only local water supply system in the Nation owned and operated by the Corps. Ownership of local water supply is best carried out by a State or local government, or by the private sector where there are appropriate market and regulatory incentives. Selling the Aqueduct to a public or private utility would contribute to American prosperity through a more efficient allocation of economic resources.

Accelerates Water Resources Infrastructure Delivery

The Budget again calls on the Congress to extend section 1043 of the Water Resources Reform and Development Act of 2014, as amended to enable non-Federal sponsors who believe they can construct projects more efficiently to do so. The Budget provides $250 million for construction of projects under this authority and $250 million for Innovative Funding Partnerships accelerating completion of projects.

Promotes Good Stewardship of Taxpayer Dollars

Increases Accountability. The Budget establishes clear priorities based on objective criteria for investment decisions. This approach ensures the best overall use of available funds and allows the American taxpayer to understand how Federal resources are allocated. For example, the Budget funds dam safety studies within the Investigations account, instead of the Operation and Maintenance account, where they appropriately belong. The Budget also makes clear to the American people when major Federal investments, in some cases started years ago, will be completed.

Increases Fiscal Discipline and Transparency. The Budget reproposes revisions to the appropriations language for the Construction, Operation and Maintenance, and Mississippi River and Tributaries accounts, and new appropriations language for the Harbor Maintenance and Inland Waterways Trust Funds, to provide greater transparency in how these funds are spent. Establishing separate appropriations accounts for the navigation trust funds would improve accountability, ensure appropriations are used for the purpose and at the level which the Congress intended, and increase transparency for the public, including the users that pay fees to finance some of these costs.

ENVIRONMENTAL PROTECTION AGENCY

Funding Highlights:

- The Environmental Protection Agency (EPA) works to protect human health and the environment by implementing and enforcing America's environmental laws.

- The 2021 Budget continues to support EPA's core work to ensure clean air, water, land, and safer chemicals and advances work on key priority areas, while reigning in unnecessary spending.

- The Budget would eliminate almost 50 wasteful programs that are outside of EPA's core mission or duplicative of other efforts, saving taxpayers over $600 million. For example, EPA's Beaches Program funds State-run beach monitoring programs, which are now established and can continue to be implemented at the local level.

- The President's 2021 Budget requests $6.7 billion for EPA, a $2.4 billion or 26-percent decrease from the 2020 enacted level.

The President's 2021 Budget:

EPA supports a safe environment and a healthy Nation by helping to provide Americans with clean air, land, and water, and ensuring chemical safety. The Budget prioritizes innovative action to address priority environmental issues, such as contamination with lead and per- and polyfluoroalkyl substances (PFAS).

Environmental protection must go hand-in-hand with a strong economy, as proven by America's continued improvements to air quality and public health while simultaneously growing the economy. The Budget promotes stewardship of taxpayer resources by reducing wasteful spending on duplicative programs and ensuring that grants are targeted effectively. Key deregulatory efforts, such as the implementation of Waters of the United States definitional changes, will reduce burden and create more certainty for American businesses. EPA's water infrastructure and clean-up programs will continue to spur investment and economic development while ensuring a safe environment for all Americans.

Prioritizes Essential EPA Functions. The 2021 Budget takes an efficient, effective approach to prioritize EPA's key responsibilities under the Nation's environmental statutes. Through cooperation with States and Tribes, local governments, businesses, and the public, EPA will continue to help provide safe drinking water, support attainment of national air quality standards, clean

Addressing PFAS

Per- and polyfluoroalkyl substances (PFAS) are a group of synthetic substances that have been widely used in industrial and consumer uses, such as non-stick cookware, water-repellent clothing, stain resistant fabrics and carpets, cosmetics, firefighting foams, and products that resist oil. Because these chemicals do not readily degrade, legacy contamination means that most people have come in contact with these compounds throughout their lifetime. EPA remains committed to supporting States, Tribes, and local communities in addressing challenges with remediating PFAS and understanding the effects to human health. The Budget provides an additional $6 million to address actions identified in *EPA's Per- and Polyfluoroalkyl Substances (PFAS) Action Plan*, such as continuing research and development to identify, test, and understand PFAS compounds, addressing current contamination issues and preventing future PFAS contamination, and effectively communicating these findings with the public.

up the Nation's most complex hazardous waste sites, ensure the safety of chemicals in the marketplace, and conduct cutting-edge environmental research.

Establishes a Lead Exposure Reduction Initiative. Millions of American families currently live in residences that can expose children to hazardous levels of lead through sources such as contaminated drinking water, household lead paint, and lead-contaminated soil. Children may also be exposed to lead in older schools. The Administration's Federal Lead Action Plan has set the stage to combat the multiple sources of this threat through commonsense solutions. The Budget would help to implement this plan through $61 million in funding to support lead testing in schools, replacement of lead pipes, certification of lead paint professionals, and development of improved lead sampling and treatment methods.

Invests in Water Infrastructure for the Future. Funding for water infrastructure remains a priority in the Budget. EPA's State Revolving Funds are funded at nearly $2 billion, which would supplement more than $80 billion currently revolving at the State level. In addition, $25 million in funding for the Water Infrastructure Finance and Innovation Act of 2014 (WIFIA) credit program could support more than $2 billion in direct loans, resulting in more than $4 billion in total water infrastructure investment. To date, the WIFIA program has issued 14 loans totaling $3.5 billion in direct credit assistance. Further, the Budget requests more than $116 million in grant funding for programs authorized in both the America's Water Infrastructure Act of 2018 and the Water Infrastructure Improvements for the Nation Act. These grants would support a wide variety of programs to address drinking water and wastewater issues including lead contamination and sewer overflows.

Reduces Burden on Taxpayer Resources through User Fees. The 2021 Budget outlines commonsense legislative proposals to authorize EPA to administer several programs through the collection and expenditure of user fees. Administering select EPA programs using funds collected from user fees would reduce the burden on taxpayer resources. Entities benefiting from those programs would directly pay for the services and benefits that the programs provide. The Budget continues to propose to fee-fund the ENERGY STAR program, along with an authorization to fee-fund compliance assistance services related to risk management, spill prevention, and response planning at industrial facilities.

Supports Revitalization of Opportunity Zones. The Budget would provide $80 million for grants to support assessment and remediation of brownfields—sites where development is complicated by prior contamination. A portion of this amount would be set aside specifically for projects in Qualified Opportunity Zones, ensuring that these resources are targeted to the communities where they can have the greatest impact. Cleaning up brownfields sites leverages other sources of investment in these communities and promotes redevelopment and economic revitalization. For example, in Detroit's New Center District, brownfields grants allowed the Detroit-Wayne County Port Authority to invest $915,000 to clean up contaminated soils, remove underground storage tanks, and eliminate vapor intrusion in a once-blighted neighborhood located in an Opportunity Zone. This investment leveraged tax credits and other incentives from the State, city and county to redevelop the site into a $28 million medical supply facility that now employs 140 workers.

Promotes Innovative Approaches to Counter or Prevent Harmful Algal Blooms. Nonpoint nutrient pollution remains a significant challenge to water quality and can trigger harmful algal blooms that endanger human health and result in significant economic impact, such as the bloom that endangered drinking water supplies in Toledo, Ohio. In recognition of this problem, the Budget includes EPA funding for harmful algal bloom predictive tools, research, and nutrient trading initiatives. In addition, the Budget proposes $15 million for a new targeted grant program to help prevent or respond to harmful algal blooms. For example, the grant could fund water testing efforts and water supply protection measures.

The Future of Detecting Airborne and Radiological Environmental Threats

In the wake of the terrorist attacks on September 11, 2001, the Federal Government developed the Airborne Spectral Photometric Environmental Collection Technology (ASPECT). ASPECT is a single engine turboprop aircraft equipped with a suite of sensors and software that uses remote hazard detection to image, map, identify, and quantify chemical vapors and deposited radioisotopes. This information is used by first responders during natural disasters, environmental emergencies, emergency responses, homeland security missions, and environmental surveys. As the technology becomes obsolete, EPA must look to the future and plan for a replacement. The 2021 Budget includes $1 million for EPA to crowdsource replacement ideas utilizing the https://challenge.gov website and framework.

NATIONAL AERONAUTICS AND SPACE ADMINISTRATION

Funding Highlights:

- The National Aeronautics and Space Administration (NASA) is responsible for leading an innovative program of exploration that would return American astronauts to the Moon by 2024 and build a sustainable presence on the lunar surface as the first steps on a journey that will take America to Mars.

- The Budget increases funding for innovative programs that would land astronauts on the Moon and support precursor missions and advanced technologies that would enable further exploration. The Budget also supports a broad range of high-performing NASA programs that are not directly supporting the Moon to Mars program, and includes reductions to some lower-performing programs.

- The Budget eliminates the Stratospheric Observatory for Infrared Astronomy (SOFIA) telescope, saving taxpayers more than $80 million per year. SOFIA is an expensive telescope mounted on a 747 airplane that is less scientifically productive than other missions with similar costs.

- The Budget provides $25.2 billion for NASA, a 12-percent increase from the 2020 enacted level.

The President's 2021 Budget:

NASA's top-priority mission is to return American astronauts to the Moon by 2024 and build a sustainable presence on the lunar surface as the first step on a journey that will take America to Mars. The Budget provides robust funding for the programs that support this goal, including $3.4 billion for the development of lander systems, over $700 million to support lunar surface activities, and $233 million for robotic precursor missions to Mars that would also conduct cutting-edge science. The Budget also funds a broad range of other NASA programs, including supporting enhanced commercial activities in Earth orbit, exciting space science missions, and research to improve air travel and remotely piloted aircraft. The Budget redirects funds from lower priority programs to fulfill the President's promise to get Americans back to the Moon.

Invests in the Systems that Would Send Astronauts to the Moon and Beyond. The Budget funds key components of NASA's Moon to Mars campaign, including: the Space Launch System (SLS) and the Orion crew capsule to support a first uncrewed test launch and a steady crewed launch cadence thereafter; the Lunar Gateway, a small way station around the Moon; commercial launch capabilities to enable regular, low-cost access to the lunar vicinity and surface; and commercial lunar landers to enable cargo delivery and human access to the lunar surface. The Gateway and landers would be launched on competitively procured vehicles, complementing crew transport flights on the SLS and Orion. The Budget defers funding of upgrades—known as "Block 1B"—for the SLS, and instead focuses the program on completing the initial version of the SLS and ensuring a reliable SLS and Orion annual flight cadence. While a potentially beneficial future capability, the costly Block 1B upgrades are not needed to land astronauts on the Moon.

> "This time, we will not only plant our flag and leave our footprint, we will establish a foundation for an eventual mission to Mars. And perhaps, someday, to many worlds beyond."
>
> President Donald J. Trump
> December 11, 2017

Funds the Development of Technologies and Early Missions Needed to Make Exploration Missions Sustainable. The Budget funds the Lunar Surface Innovation Initiative to pioneer new approaches for sustainable human exploration, including technologies to generate power, excavate and construct structures on the Moon, and help astronauts live off the land. In addition, the Budget supports an array of new prizes and challenges, research grants, and public-private partnerships to develop new technologies that would make future missions to Mars more affordable and capable. The Budget also funds the robotic exploration of Mars, in cooperation with international partners, as a precursor to human exploration. In addition to performing cutting-edge scientific investigations, a new Mars Ice Mapper mission would provide data for potential landing sites, and a Mars Sample Return mission would demonstrate the ability to launch from Mars' surface.

Supports a Long-Term American Presence in Low Earth Orbit. The Budget continues support for operations in low Earth orbit, including for new space stations that would ensure America has access to affordable space stations in the future. The Budget also funds continued use of commercial services to deliver cargo to space, American crew transportation services that would launch from American soil starting in 2020, and a range of launch, communications, rocket testing, and astronaut training capabilities that support human spaceflight.

> "[A]t the President's direction...we've put an end to decades of budget cuts and decline. And we've renewed America's commitment to human space exploration, vowing to go further into space, farther and faster than ever before."
>
> Michael R. Pence
> Vice President
> August 20, 2019

Funds Research to Make Air Travel Faster and Cheaper and Safely Integrate Drones into the Nation's Airspace. The Budget supports aeronautics research that contributes to the Nation's technological leadership and supports high-quality jobs. The Budget funds the X-59 Quiet Supersonic Technology flight demonstrator, which would fly for the first time in 2022. The Budget also increases funding for investments in ultra-fast hypersonic flight, hybrid-electric jet engine systems that could power future passenger airliners, and research on the safe integration of remotely-piloted aircraft into U.S. airspace.

Redirects Funds from Lower Priority Science and Education Programs to Higher Priorities. Consistent with prior budgets, the Budget provides no funding for the Wide Field Infrared Survey Telescope, two Earth science missions, and the Office of Science, Technology, Engineering, and Mathematics (STEM) Engagement. The Budget continues to support education activities such as internships and fellowships funded outside of the Office of STEM Engagement. The Budget also proposes to terminate the SOFIA telescope, which has not proven to be as scientifically productive as other missions.

Improves NASA's Mission Support Services. The Budget realigns budget authority and lines of reporting to free up resources for reinvestment in facilities, information technology, and other key mission support areas. The new structure supports a more efficient operating model by integrating mission support functions across geographic locations to standardize services and eliminate duplicative capabilities among NASA Centers.

SMALL BUSINESS ADMINISTRATION

Funding Highlights:

- The Small Business Administration (SBA) serves American entrepreneurs in their pursuit to start, grow, recover, and expand their businesses. As the Nation's leading advocate for small businesses, SBA ensures that business owners have access to affordable capital, mentoring and counseling opportunities, and immediate support in the wake of disaster.

- The Budget recognizes the contributions small businesses play in fostering economic growth and spurring innovation throughout the Nation. The Budget supports Boots to Business, a program that provides entrepreneurial training courses to veterans, servicemembers transitioning from military to civilian life, and military spouses through the Department of Defense's Transition Assistance Program (TAP).

- The Budget continues to demonstrate fiscal restraint by prioritizing the essential functions of the Federal Government and cutting wasteful or duplicative programs. The Budget eliminates funding for the Program for Investment in Micro-Entrepreneurs (PRIME). These services are already provided by SBA's Microloan Technical Assistance Program. Eliminating PRIME would save taxpayers $6 million a year based on the 2020 enacted level.

- The Budget requests $739 million in new budget authority for 2021, a $243 million or 25-percent decrease from the 2020 enacted level, which includes funds provided under the disaster relief cap. This request is partially offset by a fiscally responsible proposal to allow SBA the flexibility to set an upfront fee across its business loan programs, providing $80 million in offsetting collections.

The President's 2021 Budget:

Small businesses are the engines of the American economy. They are the job creators and innovators that fuel American neighborhoods and preserve U.S. prosperity. The SBA was established in 1953 to aid, counsel, assist, and protect the interests of small business concerns; preserve free competitive enterprise; and maintain and strengthen the overall economy of the Nation. Today, SBA continues to support the Nation's 30 million small businesses through an array of tailored programs and services. SBA's lending programs complement credit markets by meeting demand when credit-worthy small business borrowers cannot obtain financing on reasonable terms or conditions. Its nationwide network of private-sector and non-profit partners educate, advise, and inspire a new generation of entrepreneurs. In 2021, SBA will be uniquely positioned to leverage the Administration's pro-growth policies to equip small business owners with the right resources to be competitive in today's market and promote economic security for their businesses and families. The Agency will fulfill this mission while promoting fiscal discipline by proposing policies that level the playing field with private sector support for small businesses.

Expands Opportunity for Small Business Owners. The Budget supports $43 billion in business lending to assist U.S. small business owners in accessing affordable capital to start, build, and grow their businesses. These products serve a variety of business needs, from funding general business operations, such as working capital and capital expenses, to fixed-asset financing for machinery and equipment, construction, and commercial real estate. They also provide the opportunity for small businesses to refinance existing loans. To ensure that SBA can provide these services at the least cost to taxpayers, the Budget proposes that SBA set an upfront administrative fee across its business loan programs to levels necessary to offset a portion of the costs of providing this assistance.

> *"America's 30 million small businesses are central to our economy and our communities. Their courageous innovation makes our cities and towns vibrant places to live, work, and raise families."*
>
> President Donald J. Trump
> May 3, 2019

Promotes Investment Opportunities for Microborrowers. Through its 7(m) Direct Microloan program, the SBA supports low-interest financing for non-profit intermediaries that in turn provide loans of up to $50,000 small businesses and startups. In addition to the $25 million in technical assistance grant funds requested for the Microloan program, the Budget requests $4 million to support $41 million in direct lending. These efforts would support more than 20,000 jobs and spur economic growth throughout the Nation.

Supports Economic Recovery Efforts in the Wake of Disaster. SBA continues to be a vital resource for American households and businesses that need to recover quickly following disasters. In 2019, SBA approved more than 42,000 disaster loans totaling over $2.2 billion in direct, low-interest lending to business owners, homeowners, renters, and property owners. The Budget provides continued support for these efforts, and includes new information technology investments that would improve customer service and reduce the burden on disaster survivors.

Promotes Effective and Accountable Grant Funding. SBA leverages its nationwide field personnel and diverse network of private sector and non-profit resource partners across each State and Territory to provide counseling, mentoring, and training assistance to nearly one million small business owners each year. The Budget continues to propose changes to the Small Business Development Center program to create a competitive set-aside to reward partners that most efficiently serve small businesses and to grant the authority to collect limited grantee data for internal program evaluation purposes. The Budget also proposes funding to support the implementation of additional Boots to Business program training sessions through the Department of Defense's TAP program.

Creates Opportunities in Federal Contracting. The Federal Government is the largest producer of goods and services in the world. SBA provides oversight in Federal contracting to ensure the Government meets or exceeds the minimum set-aside of 23 percent for small businesses. Access to these funding opportunities enables small businesses to provide innovative solutions, drive economic growth, and support their communities. The Budget continues to invest in SBA's 8(a) program to establish a full certification program for SBA's women-owned business certification programs.

> *"I am passionate about empowering entrepreneurs of all backgrounds and ethnicities with the guidance and the support needed to achieve success."*
>
> Jovita Carranza
> Administrator (as Nominee)
> December 11, 2019

Summary Tables

Table S–1. Budget Totals

(In billions of dollars and as a percent of GDP)

	2019	2020	2021	2022	2023	2024	2025	2026	2027	2028	2029	2030	Totals 2021–2025	Totals 2021–2030
Budget Totals in Billions of Dollars:														
Receipts	3,464	3,706	3,863	4,086	4,359	4,657	4,924	5,182	5,455	5,762	6,059	6,378	21,889	50,725
Outlays	4,448	4,790	4,829	5,005	5,105	5,208	5,451	5,663	5,891	6,236	6,309	6,639	25,599	56,338
Deficit	984	1,083	966	920	746	552	527	481	435	475	250	261	3,711	5,613
Debt held by the public	16,801	17,881	18,912	19,891	20,688	21,284	21,848	22,362	22,826	23,327	23,604	23,892		
Gross domestic product (GDP)	21,216	22,211	23,353	24,543	25,791	27,104	28,473	29,884	31,343	32,875	34,480	36,164		
Budget Totals as a Percent of GDP:														
Receipts	16.3%	16.7%	16.5%	16.6%	16.9%	17.2%	17.3%	17.3%	17.4%	17.5%	17.6%	17.6%	16.9%	17.2%
Outlays	21.0%	21.6%	20.7%	20.4%	19.8%	19.2%	19.1%	19.0%	18.8%	19.0%	18.3%	18.4%	19.8%	19.3%
Deficit	4.6%	4.9%	4.1%	3.7%	2.9%	2.0%	1.8%	1.6%	1.4%	1.4%	0.7%	0.7%	2.9%	2.1%
Debt held by the public	79.2%	80.5%	81.0%	81.0%	80.2%	78.5%	76.7%	74.8%	72.8%	71.0%	68.5%	66.1%		

Table S–2.　Effect of Budget Proposals on Projected Deficits

(Deficit increases (+) or decreases (–) in billions of dollars)

	2019	2020	2021	2022	2023	2024	2025	2026	2027	2028	2029	2030	Totals 2021–2025	Totals 2021–2030
Projected deficits in the baseline	984	1,085	1,014	1,047	958	851	922	997	1,039	1,180	1,038	1,192	4,793	10,239
Percent of GDP	4.6%	4.9%	4.3%	4.3%	3.7%	3.1%	3.2%	3.3%	3.3%	3.6%	3.0%	3.3%		
Proposals in the 2021 Budget:														
Invest in critical national priorities:														
Provide defense funding to support the National Defense Strategy[1]			3	31	36	40	43	35	21	5	–14	–34	153	166
Support major investment in infrastructure			5	24	38	47	38	19	10	5	5		152	190
Reauthorize surface transportation programs[2]			1	3	4	5	7	8	10	11	13	14	20	75
Establish a Federal Capital Revolving Fund			*	2	2	2	2	*	*	*	*		8	9
Establish Education Freedom Scholarships			1	5	5	5	5	5	5	5	5	5	21	45
Provide paid parental leave			1	1	1	2	2	2	3	3	3	3	7	21
Debt service			*	1	2	4	6	9	12	14	15	15	13	78
Total			10	66	88	106	103	79	59	42	26	4	374	585
Restrain spending to protect and respect American taxpayers:														
Rightsize Government and apply two-penny plan to non-defense discretionary spending[3]		*	–3	–37	–79	–113	–146	–176	–205	–234	–264	–293	–378	–1,550
Reflect phase down of Overseas Contingency Operations funding[3]			–2	–31	–47	–59	–65	–69	–71	–73	–75	–76	–204	–567
Advance the President's health reform vision[4]		1	8	–2	–33	–38	–76	–80	–84	–105	–98	–88	–141	–597
Modernize Medicaid and the Children's Health Insurance Program (CHIP)			–8	–16	–17	–18	–19	–20	–21	–22	–25	–26	–78	–193
Address wasteful spending, fraud, and abuse in healthcare			–9	–25	–32	–39	–49	–60	–65	–71	–76	–83	–154	–509
Enact comprehensive drug pricing reform			–1	–5	–6	–12	–13	–18	–18	–21	–21	–21	–37	–135
Reform welfare programs			–20	–27	–28	–29	–30	–31	–31	–31	–33	–33	–134	–292
Reform Federal student loans			–6	–11	–15	–18	–19	–19	–20	–20	–21	–21	–69	–170
Reform Federal disability programs and improve payment integrity			–1	–2	–2	–2	–3	–6	–9	–13	–16	–21	–10	–76
Modify retirement and health benefits for Federal employees			–2	–1	–4	–7	–9	–11	–12	–13	–14	–16	–24	–89
Implement agricultural reforms			–2	–5	–4	–7	–6	–6	–6	–6	–7	–7	–24	–56
Reform the Postal Service		–2		–7	–8	–11	–13	–6	–7	–13	–11	–15	–39	–91
Other spending reductions, program reforms, and adjustments			–7	–21	–17	–33	–39	–54	–54	–48	–53	–113	–117	–436
Debt service and other interest effects			–1	–3	–7	–13	–24	–39	–58	–79	–101	–125	–47	–450
Total		–1	–59	–193	–301	–405	–498	–595	–663	–748	–814	–935	–1,456	–5,211
Total proposals in the 2021 Budget		–1	–48	–127	–212	–299	–395	–515	–604	–705	–788	–931	–1,082	–4,626
Resulting deficits in the 2021 Budget	984	1,083	966	920	746	552	527	481	435	475	250	261	3,711	5,613
Percent of GDP	4.6%	4.9%	4.1%	3.7%	2.9%	2.0%	1.8%	1.6%	1.4%	1.4%	0.7%	0.7%		

* $500 million or less.

[1] The 2021 Budget proposes to fund base defense programs for 2021 at the current law level, and provides an increase in defense funding of about two percent each year through 2025. After 2025, the Budget includes placeholder levels frozen at the 2025 level; these notional levels are compared to the statutorily required inflated baseline, which accounts for the reductions in the outyears.

[2] Represents the resources required to fund the policy proposal for the Highway Trust Fund above the inflated baseline. The full policy funds a 10-year, $810 billion reauthorization.

[3] Net of spending in the inflated baseline.

[4] Net of adjustments. See S–6 for more details.

Table S–3. Baseline by Category[1]
(In billions of dollars)

	2019	2020	2021	2022	2023	2024	2025	2026	2027	2028	2029	2030	Totals 2021–2025	Totals 2021–2030
Outlays:														
Discretionary programs:														
Defense	676	713	753	769	782	797	812	829	850	870	891	913	3,913	8,267
Non-defense	661	724	733	748	758	774	784	801	816	835	853	873	3,797	7,975
Subtotal, discretionary programs	1,338	1,438	1,486	1,516	1,541	1,571	1,596	1,630	1,665	1,705	1,744	1,786	7,710	16,242
Mandatory programs:														
Social Security	1,038	1,092	1,151	1,217	1,287	1,362	1,442	1,526	1,615	1,709	1,807	1,909	6,459	15,026
Medicare	644	694	746	828	847	864	973	1,043	1,114	1,273	1,222	1,399	4,259	10,310
Medicaid	409	447	452	474	502	526	556	594	628	665	711	754	2,509	5,861
Other mandatory programs	644	744	660	694	698	700	740	787	811	872	849	914	3,493	7,726
Subtotal, mandatory programs	2,735	2,977	3,010	3,212	3,334	3,453	3,711	3,950	4,168	4,520	4,590	4,976	16,720	38,923
Net interest	375	376	379	401	434	469	518	575	633	686	731	775	2,201	5,601
Total outlays	4,448	4,791	4,875	5,130	5,308	5,493	5,826	6,154	6,466	6,911	7,065	7,538	26,631	60,765
Receipts:														
Individual income taxes	1,718	1,812	1,929	2,047	2,181	2,340	2,497	2,668	2,849	3,026	3,213	3,409	10,995	26,159
Corporation income taxes	230	264	284	324	382	426	447	435	430	443	446	453	1,864	4,070
Social insurance and retirement receipts:														
Social Security payroll taxes	914	967	1,011	1,065	1,116	1,175	1,234	1,301	1,363	1,441	1,510	1,586	5,601	12,802
Medicare payroll taxes	278	292	308	326	343	361	380	401	422	447	469	494	1,718	3,952
Unemployment insurance	41	42	43	44	44	46	47	50	52	53	54	56	224	489
Other retirement	10	11	11	12	13	13	14	14	15	16	17	18	63	142
Excise taxes	99	95	87	89	90	95	95	97	98	99	102	105	457	959
Estate and gift taxes	17	20	22	23	24	26	28	29	31	33	35	37	122	286
Customs duties	71	92	54	43	44	45	47	48	49	50	52	52	232	484
Deposits of earnings, Federal Reserve System	53	73	71	68	68	67	64	61	62	64	68	74	338	667
Other miscellaneous receipts	33	39	40	42	44	47	50	54	57	59	61	62	224	516
Total receipts	3,464	3,706	3,860	4,083	4,350	4,642	4,904	5,158	5,427	5,731	6,027	6,346	21,838	50,526
Deficit	**984**	**1,085**	**1,014**	**1,047**	**958**	**851**	**922**	**997**	**1,039**	**1,180**	**1,038**	**1,192**	**4,793**	**10,239**
Net interest	375	376	379	401	434	469	518	575	633	686	731	775	2,201	5,601
Primary deficit	609	708	635	646	525	383	404	422	406	494	307	417	2,592	4,639
On-budget deficit	992	1,092	1,006	1,025	919	799	852	922	949	1,082	917	1,052	4,601	9,524
Off-budget deficit/surplus (–)	–8	–7	8	22	39	53	69	74	90	99	121	140	192	715
Memorandum, budget authority for discretionary programs:														
Defense	719	746	753	771	789	808	828	848	868	889	911	933	3,949	8,398
Non-defense	658	671	655	671	688	705	722	740	758	777	796	815	3,442	7,326
Total, discretionary budget authority	1,377	1,417	1,408	1,442	1,477	1,513	1,550	1,587	1,626	1,666	1,707	1,748	7,390	15,724

[1] Baseline estimates are on the basis of the economic assumptions shown in Table S–9, which incorporate the effects of the Administration's fiscal policies.

Table S–4. Proposed Budget by Category

(In billions of dollars)

	2019	2020	2021	2022	2023	2024	2025	2026	2027	2028	2029	2030	Totals 2021-2025	Totals 2021-2030
Outlays:														
Discretionary programs:														
Defense	676	713	754	769	771	778	790	796	800	802	803	803	3,862	7,866
Non-defense	661	725	732	708	678	659	638	626	612	603	595	587	3,414	6,438
Subtotal, discretionary programs	1,338	1,438	1,485	1,477	1,449	1,437	1,428	1,421	1,412	1,406	1,397	1,391	7,277	14,304
Mandatory programs:														
Social Security	1,038	1,092	1,151	1,216	1,286	1,361	1,440	1,523	1,611	1,706	1,804	1,906	6,453	15,002
Medicare	644	694	722	779	790	799	899	961	1,026	1,178	1,132	1,269	3,989	9,554
Medicaid	409	447	448	449	450	452	453	477	505	531	570	607	2,252	4,941
Other mandatory programs	644	743	645	686	703	701	733	738	751	796	762	802	3,467	7,315
Subtotal, mandatory programs	2,735	2,975	2,966	3,130	3,228	3,313	3,524	3,698	3,893	4,210	4,267	4,583	16,161	36,813
Net interest	375	376	378	399	428	458	499	543	586	621	645	665	2,161	5,221
Total outlays	4,448	4,790	4,829	5,005	5,105	5,208	5,451	5,663	5,891	6,236	6,309	6,639	25,599	56,338
Receipts:														
Individual income taxes	1,718	1,812	1,932	2,048	2,185	2,346	2,505	2,679	2,862	3,040	3,228	3,426	11,016	26,251
Corporation income taxes	230	264	284	324	382	426	448	435	431	443	446	453	1,865	4,073
Social insurance and retirement receipts:														
Social Security payroll taxes	914	967	1,011	1,065	1,116	1,174	1,234	1,300	1,362	1,441	1,510	1,586	5,600	12,798
Medicare payroll taxes	278	292	308	326	342	361	380	401	422	447	469	494	1,718	3,951
Unemployment insurance	41	42	43	44	46	48	50	52	54	56	57	57	230	507
Other retirement	10	11	11	14	17	20	23	25	27	29	30	31	86	229
Excise taxes	99	95	87	89	90	95	95	97	98	99	102	105	457	959
Estate and gift taxes	17	20	22	23	24	26	28	29	31	33	35	37	122	286
Customs duties	71	92	54	43	44	45	47	48	49	50	52	52	232	484
Deposits of earnings, Federal Reserve System	53	73	71	69	68	68	64	62	62	65	69	74	340	673
Other miscellaneous receipts	33	39	40	42	44	47	50	53	56	59	61	62	223	513
Total receipts	3,464	3,706	3,863	4,086	4,359	4,657	4,924	5,182	5,455	5,762	6,059	6,378	21,889	50,725
Deficit	**984**	**1,083**	**966**	**920**	**746**	**552**	**527**	**481**	**435**	**475**	**250**	**261**	**3,711**	**5,613**
Net interest	375	376	378	399	428	458	499	543	586	621	645	665	2,161	5,221
Primary deficit/surplus (–)	609	707	588	521	319	94	27	-62	-150	-146	-395	-404	1,549	392
On-budget deficit	992	1,091	959	900	708	501	460	411	350	381	134	127	3,527	4,929
Off-budget deficit/surplus (–)	-8	-7	7	20	38	51	67	71	86	94	116	134	183	684
Memorandum, budget authority for discretionary programs:														
Defense	719	746	741	759	775	791	808	808	808	808	808	808	3,874	7,914
Non-defense	658	672	595	583	572	559	547	536	525	514	505	495	2,855	5,430
Total, discretionary budget authority	1,377	1,418	1,336	1,342	1,347	1,350	1,355	1,344	1,333	1,322	1,313	1,303	6,729	13,344

Table S–5. Proposed Budget by Category as a Percent of GDP

(As a percent of GDP)

	2019	2020	2021	2022	2023	2024	2025	2026	2027	2028	2029	2030	Averages 2021-2025	Averages 2021-2030
Outlays:														
Discretionary programs:														
Defense	3.2	3.2	3.2	3.1	3.0	2.9	2.8	2.7	2.6	2.4	2.3	2.2	3.0	2.7
Non-defense	3.1	3.3	3.1	2.9	2.6	2.4	2.2	2.1	2.0	1.8	1.7	1.6	2.7	2.3
Subtotal, discretionary programs	6.3	6.5	6.4	6.0	5.6	5.3	5.0	4.8	4.5	4.3	4.1	3.8	5.7	5.0
Mandatory programs:														
Social Security	4.9	4.9	4.9	5.0	5.0	5.0	5.1	5.1	5.1	5.2	5.2	5.3	5.0	5.1
Medicare	3.0	3.1	3.1	3.2	3.1	2.9	3.2	3.2	3.3	3.6	3.3	3.5	3.1	3.2
Medicaid	1.9	2.0	1.9	1.8	1.8	1.7	1.6	1.6	1.6	1.6	1.7	1.7	1.8	1.7
Other mandatory programs	3.0	3.3	2.8	2.8	2.7	2.6	2.6	2.5	2.4	2.4	2.2	2.2	2.7	2.5
Subtotal, mandatory programs	12.9	13.4	12.7	12.8	12.5	12.2	12.4	12.4	12.4	12.8	12.4	12.7	12.5	12.5
Net interest	1.8	1.7	1.6	1.6	1.7	1.7	1.8	1.8	1.9	1.9	1.9	1.8	1.7	1.8
Total outlays	21.0	21.6	20.7	20.4	19.8	19.2	19.1	19.0	18.8	19.0	18.3	18.4	19.8	19.3
Receipts:														
Individual income taxes	8.1	8.2	8.3	8.3	8.5	8.7	8.8	9.0	9.1	9.2	9.4	9.5	8.5	8.9
Corporation income taxes	1.1	1.2	1.2	1.3	1.5	1.6	1.6	1.5	1.4	1.3	1.3	1.3	1.4	1.4
Social insurance and retirement receipts:														
Social Security payroll taxes	4.3	4.4	4.3	4.3	4.3	4.3	4.3	4.4	4.3	4.4	4.4	4.4	4.3	4.4
Medicare payroll taxes	1.3	1.3	1.3	1.3	1.3	1.3	1.3	1.3	1.3	1.4	1.4	1.4	1.3	1.3
Unemployment insurance	0.2	0.2	0.2	0.2	0.2	0.2	0.2	0.2	0.2	0.2	0.1	0.2	0.2	0.2
Other retirement	*	*	*	0.1	0.1	0.1	0.1	0.1	0.1	0.1	0.1	0.1	0.1	0.1
Excise taxes	0.5	0.4	0.4	0.4	0.4	0.4	0.3	0.3	0.3	0.3	0.3	0.3	0.4	0.3
Estate and gift taxes	0.1	0.1	0.1	0.1	0.1	0.1	0.1	0.1	0.1	0.1	0.1	0.1	0.1	0.1
Customs duties	0.3	0.4	0.2	0.2	0.2	0.2	0.2	0.2	0.2	0.2	0.2	0.1	0.2	0.2
Deposits of earnings, Federal Reserve System	0.2	0.3	0.3	0.3	0.3	0.3	0.2	0.2	0.2	0.2	0.2	0.2	0.3	0.2
Other miscellaneous receipts	0.2	0.2	0.2	0.2	0.2	0.2	0.2	0.2	0.2	0.2	0.2	0.2	0.2	0.2
Total receipts	16.3	16.7	16.5	16.6	16.9	17.2	17.3	17.3	17.4	17.5	17.6	17.6	16.9	17.2
Deficit	**4.6**	**4.9**	**4.1**	**3.7**	**2.9**	**2.0**	**1.8**	**1.6**	**1.4**	**1.4**	**0.7**	**0.7**	**2.9**	**2.1**
Net interest	1.8	1.7	1.6	1.6	1.7	1.7	1.8	1.8	1.9	1.9	1.9	1.8	1.7	1.8
Primary deficit/surplus (–)	2.9	3.2	2.5	2.1	1.2	0.3	0.1	-0.2	-0.5	-0.4	-1.1	-1.1	1.3	0.3
On-budget deficit	4.7	4.9	4.1	3.7	2.7	1.8	1.6	1.4	1.1	1.2	0.4	0.4	2.8	1.8
Off-budget deficit/surplus (–)	–*	–*	*	0.1	0.1	0.2	0.2	0.2	0.3	0.3	0.3	0.4	0.1	0.2
Memorandum, budget authority for discretionary programs:														
Defense	3.4	3.4	3.2	3.1	3.1	2.9	2.8	2.7	2.6	2.5	2.3	2.2	3.0	2.7
Non-defense	3.1	3.0	2.5	2.4	2.2	2.1	1.9	1.8	1.7	1.6	1.5	1.4	2.2	1.9
Total, discretionary budget authority	6.5	6.4	5.7	5.5	5.2	5.0	4.8	4.5	4.3	4.0	3.8	3.6	5.2	4.6

*0.05 percent of GDP or less

Table S-6. Mandatory and Receipt Proposals

(Deficit increases (+) or decreases (–) in millions of dollars)

	2020	2021	2022	2023	2024	2025	2026	2027	2028	2029	2030	Totals 2021–2025	Totals 2021–2030
Mandatory Initiatives and Savings:													
Agriculture:													
Tighten farm payment eligibility rules		−212	−260	−273	−261	−249	−258	−284	−276	−291	−290	−1,255	−2,654
Reduce Crop Insurance subsidies		−12	−2,151	−2,177	−2,806	−2,853	−2,903	−2,953	−2,998	−3,047	−3,085	−9,999	−24,985
Eliminate redundant Farm Bill programs		−583	−650	−665	−621	−632	−641	−648	−658	−660	−659	−3,151	−6,417
Streamline conservation programs		−215	−427	−672	−892	−1,094	−1,131	−1,171	−1,181	−1,181	−1,181	−3,300	−9,145
Eliminate in-kind international food aid		−166	−166	−166	−166	−166	−166	−166	−166	−166	−166	−830	−1,660
Establish new user fees for food inspection and mineral extraction		−30	−675	−660	−660	−660	−660	−660	−660	−660	−660	−2,685	−5,985
Reform commodity purchases under Section 32		−415	−436	−457	−479	−502	−524	−546	−570	−594	−618	−2,289	−5,141
Improve Child Nutrition program integrity		−20	−125	−155	−187	−192	−197	−202	−207	−212	−217	−679	−1,714
Total, Agriculture		−1,653	−4,890	−5,225	−6,072	−6,348	−6,480	−6,630	−6,716	−6,811	−6,876	−24,188	−57,701
Education:													
Create single income-driven student loan repayment plan [1]		−936	−3,647	−5,780	−6,845	−6,951	−6,956	−7,178	−7,151	−7,105	−7,216	−24,159	−59,765
Eliminate standard repayment cap		−1,942	−2,533	−2,682	−2,728	−2,749	−2,850	−2,929	−3,003	−3,053	−3,088	−12,634	−27,557
Use combined Adjusted Gross Income to calculate loan payments for married filing separately		−194	−321	−437	−507	−541	−554	−581	−588	−570	−607	−2,000	−4,900
Eliminate subsidized student loans		−377	−1,180	−1,663	−2,048	−2,216	−2,285	−2,229	−2,111	−2,136	−2,077	−7,484	−18,322
Eliminate Public Service Loan Forgiveness		−1,911	−3,348	−4,508	−5,265	−5,738	−5,945	−6,100	−6,198	−6,508	−6,651	−20,770	−52,172
Eliminate account maintenance fee payments to guaranty agencies		−466										−466	−466
Establish student loan risk sharing													
Limit graduate student loan borrowing		−181	−895	−1,430	−1,894	−2,361	−2,919	−3,684	−4,282	−4,723	−5,212	−6,761	−27,581
Limit parent student loan borrowing		71	467	1,126	1,804	2,258	2,559	2,820	3,039	3,247	3,454	5,726	20,845
Move Iraq-Afghanistan Service Grants into the Pell Grant program [2]													
Expand Pell Grants to short-term programs		12	29	35	41	46	46	48	48	49	51	163	405
Make incarcerated students eligible for Pell Grants		10	22	23	23	23	23	23	23	24	24	101	218
Reallocate mandatory Pell Grant funding to support expanded eligibility		893	4,847	4,928	5,006	4,974	5,036	4,916	4,934	4,960	4,994	20,648	45,488
Reduce improper payments in Pell Grants		−22	−51	−58	−64	−69	−69	−71	−71	−73	−75	−264	−623
Establish Education Freedom Scholarships [3]		−2	−4	−4	−4	−4	−4	−4	−4	−4	−4	−18	−38
Total, Education		−5,045	−6,614	−10,450	−12,481	−13,328	−13,918	−14,969	−15,364	−15,892	−16,407	−47,918	−124,468
Energy:													
Divest the Power Marketing Administrations' (PMAs)[4] transmission assets			−1,688	−364	−382	−349	−246	−254	−263	−271	−271	−2,783	−4,088
Pursue additional reforms of the PMAs		−1,297	−1,201	−693	−875	373	−749	−617	−784	−1,089	−989	−3,693	−7,921
Restart Nuclear Waste Fund fee in 2023				−346	−342	−334	−325	−325	−325	−325	−325	−1,022	−2,647
Total, Energy		−1,297	−2,889	−1,403	−1,599	−310	−1,320	−1,196	−1,372	−1,685	−1,585	−7,498	−14,656
Health and Human Services (HHS):													
Mitigate impact of Temporary Assistance for Needy Families (TANF) and Social Services Block Grant (SSBG) program changes on child care spending		221	235	212	218	217	216	216	216	216	216	1,103	2,183
Expand access to the National Directory of New Hires													

Table S–6. Mandatory and Receipt Proposals—Continued

(Deficit increases (+) or decreases (−) in millions of dollars)

	2020	2021	2022	2023	2024	2025	2026	2027	2028	2029	2030	Totals 2021–2025	Totals 2021–2030
Reauthorize Healthy Marriage and Responsible Fatherhood Grants		1	1	1	1	1	1	1	1	1	1	5	10
Increase repatriation ceiling		50	300	300	300	50						1,000	1,000
Build the supply of child care													
Establish an Unaccompanied Alien Children Contingency Fund		130	60	6	2	1	1					199	200
Fund States to provide parenting time services		1	1	2	2	2	3	3	4	4	4	8	26
Enhance and reform foster care and permanency programs		27	55	90	139	179	199	223	262	288	273	490	1,735
Expand promoting safe and stable families programs		22	136	193	130	84	80	75	70	70	70	565	930
Enact comprehensive drug pricing reform		−1,400	−5,100	−6,000	−12,000	−12,000	−17,500	−18,000	−21,000	−21,000	−21,000	−36,500	−135,000
Advance kidney care:													
Extend immunosuppressive drug coverage for kidney transplant patients [4]													
Allow the Secretary to determine the appropriate recertification period for organ procurement organizations [4]													
Allow the Secretary to determine the appropriate number of organ procurement organizations [4]													
Total, advance kidney care													
Improve access to rural healthcare:													
Modernize payment for Rural Health Clinics		−20	−60	−80	−110	−160	−200	−230	−290	−290	−350	−430	−1,790
Expand and enhance access to Medicare telehealth services [4]													
Preserve access to rural emergency hospitals [4]													
Total, improve access to rural healthcare		−20	−60	−80	−110	−160	−200	−230	−290	−290	−350	−430	−1,790
Reduce Government-imposed burden in Medicare:													
Allow beneficiaries to opt-out of Medicare Part A and retain Social Security benefits													
Give Medicare beneficiaries with high deductible health plans the option to make tax deductible contributions to health savings accounts or medical savings accounts [3]		615	1,095	1,311	1,536	1,665	1,827	1,958	2,025	2,089	2,154	6,222	16,275
Reform Medicare practitioner opt out [4]													
Modify reinsurance arrangements for Medicare Advantage plans			10	20	20	20	20	20	20	20	20	70	170
Eliminate beneficiary coinsurance for screening colonoscopies with polyp removal		310	370	400	430	460	500	530	570	610	650	1,970	4,830
Other		−150	−90	90	140	70	50	60	90	100	130	60	490
Total, reduce Government-imposed burden in Medicare		775	1,385	1,821	2,126	2,215	2,397	2,568	2,705	2,819	2,954	8,322	21,765
Eliminate wasteful Federal spending in Medicare:													
Reform graduate medical education payments [5]		530	−1,930	−2,860	−3,750	−4,720	−5,710	−6,730	−7,820	−8,990	−10,190	−12,730	−52,170
Modify payments to hospitals for uncompensated care [6]			−5,760	−7,170	−7,990	−8,870	−9,750	−10,660	−11,590	−12,570	−13,570	−29,790	−87,930
Reduce Medicare coverage of bad debts		−410	−1,230	−2,590	−3,440	−3,730	−3,950	−4,180	−4,430	−4,690	−4,950	−11,400	−33,600
Address excessive payment for post-acute care providers by establishing a unified payment system based on patients' clinical needs rather than the site of care		−1,280	−3,120	−5,140	−7,710	−11,040	−12,520	−13,530	−15,070	−15,210	−16,830	−28,290	−101,450

Table S–6. Mandatory and Receipt Proposals—Continued

(Deficit increases (+) or decreases (–) in millions of dollars)

	2020	2021	2022	2023	2024	2025	2026	2027	2028	2029	2030	Totals 2021–2025	Totals 2021–2030
Modify payment for hospice care provided to beneficiaries in skilled nursing and nursing facilities	....	–310	–330	–360	–390	–420	–450	–490	–540	–590	–640	–1,810	–4,520
Pay all hospital-owned physician offices located off-campus at the physician office rate	....	–1,800	–3,290	–3,670	–4,060	–4,480	–4,940	–5,420	–5,940	–6,500	–7,140	–17,300	–47,240
Pay on-campus hospital outpatient departments at the physician office rate for certain services	....	–4,200	–7,740	–8,710	–9,770	–10,900	–12,160	–13,550	–15,050	–16,700	–18,420	–41,320	–117,200
Other	....	–635	–815	–935	–1,630	–2,225	–2,450	–2,635	–2,870	–3,125	–3,390	–6,240	–20,710
Total, eliminate wasteful Federal spending in Medicare	....	–8,105	–24,215	–31,435	–38,740	–46,385	–51,930	–57,195	–63,310	–68,375	–75,130	–148,880	–464,820
Address fraud and abuse in Medicare	....	–732	–872	–783	–793	–823	–1,653	–1,854	–1,964	–2,054	–2,164	–4,003	–13,692
Address wasteful spending, fraud, and abuse in Medicaid:													
Strengthen the Centers for Medicare and Medicaid Services' ability to recoup Medicaid improper payments	....	....	–470	–500	–530	–560	–590	–630	–670	–710	–750	–2,060	–5,410
Continue Medicaid Disproportionate Share Hospital allotment reductions	....	....	....	....	....	....	–6,520	–6,490	–6,470	–6,450	–6,430	....	–32,360
Improve processes for recovering Federal and State overpayments	....	–75	–79	–85	–90	–95	–100	–106	–113	–119	–126	–424	–988
Strengthen and clarify State provider screening, enrollment, and termination requirements [4]	....	....	....	....	....	....	....	....	....	....	....	....	....
Other	....	–905	–945	–985	–1,036	–3,046	–1,136	–1,187	–1,247	–1,308	–1,368	–6,917	–13,163
Total, address wasteful spending, fraud, and abuse in Medicaid	....	–980	–1,494	–1,570	–1,656	–3,701	–8,346	–8,413	–8,500	–8,587	–8,674	–9,401	–51,921
Modernize Medicaid and the Children's Health Insurance Program (CHIP):													
Implement Medicaid community engagement requirement	....	–8,000	–12,600	–13,300	–14,200	–14,800	–15,600	–16,400	–17,300	–19,700	–20,500	–62,900	–152,400
Create new Money Follows the Person State plan option	....	....	86	58	42	–12	–39	–48	–57	–59	–62	174	–91
Other	....	–320	–3,410	–3,710	–3,930	–4,160	–4,440	–4,690	–4,950	–5,480	–5,810	–15,530	–40,900
Total, modernize Medicaid and CHIP	....	–8,320	–15,924	–16,952	–18,088	–18,972	–20,079	–21,138	–22,307	–25,239	–26,372	–78,256	–193,391
Address opioids and mental health in Medicaid and CHIP:													
Address Medicaid Institutions for Mental Diseases (IMD) exclusion:													
Exempt Qualified Residential Treatment Programs from Medicaid IMD payment exclusion	....	200	300	500	500	600	600	600	700	700	700	2,100	5,400
Extend Community Mental Health Services demonstration program	....	5	15	20	30	40	50	60	75	95	110	110	500
Prohibit States from terminating CHIP coverage for inmates	....	906	....	....	....	....	....	....	....	....	....	906	906
Prohibit States from terminating Medicaid coverage for inmates for six months	....	....	....	....	....	....	....	....	....	....	....	....	....
Allow States to extend Medicaid coverage for pregnant women with substance use disorder to one year postpartum	....	25	20	20	20	20	20	20	20	20	20	105	205
Total, address opioids and mental health in Medicaid and CHIP	....	1,136	335	540	550	660	670	680	795	815	830	3,221	7,011

Table S–6. Mandatory and Receipt Proposals—Continued

(Deficit increases (+) or decreases (–) in millions of dollars)

	2020	2021	2022	2023	2024	2025	2026	2027	2028	2029	2030	Totals 2021–2025	Totals 2021–2030
Extend mandatory funding and provide authorities, including tax provisions, for select public health programs:													
Extend Health Centers through 2021	641	2,555	2,134	54	40							4,783	4,783
Extend the National Health Service Corps through 2021	24	132	196	50	12	6						396	396
Extend Teaching Health Centers Graduate Medical Education through 2021	24	84	51	13								148	148
Extend the Special Diabetes Programs for the National Institutes of Health and the Indian Health Service through 2021	54	169	51	47	36	27	15	5	1	1		330	352
	5	42	53	35	31	31	29	29	29	30	30	192	339
Other													
Total, extend mandatory funding and provide authorities, including tax provisions, for select public health programs	748	2,982	2,485	199	119	64	44	34	30	31	30	5,849	6,018
Reform the Indian Health Service													
Additional health proposals:													
Reform medical liability [3]		−160	−593	−1,541	−2,511	−3,562	−4,884	−6,021	−6,799	−6,806	−7,421	−8,367	−40,298
Enforce conscience and protections against coercion in HHS programs [4]													
Protect the religious liberty of child welfare providers [4]		12	150	38								200	200
Other													
Total, additional health proposals		−148	−443	−1,503	−2,511	−3,562	−4,884	−6,021	−6,799	−6,806	−7,421	−8,167	−40,098
Medicare and Medicaid interactions		6,515	8,844	8,850	8,981	8,798	8,751	8,853	9,107	10,591	11,064	41,988	90,354
Total, Health and Human Services	748	−7,845	−34,271	−46,109	−61,330	−73,332	−92,230	−100,198	−110,980	−117,516	−125,669	−222,887	−769,480
Homeland Security:													
Adjust collection and use of customs and immigration user fees [3]		−340	−203	−225	−227	−252	−256	−286	−288	−309	−5,800	−1,247	−8,186
Establish an immigration services surcharge [3]		−389	−398	−407	−416	−426	−436	−446	−456	−466	−477	−2,036	−4,317
Increase worksite enforcement penalties [3]		−13	−14	−15	−15	−15	−15	−15	−15	−15	−15	−72	−147
Establish National Flood Insurance Program affordability assistance		5	93	132	168	200	228	253	271	284	292	598	1,926
Total, Homeland Security		−737	−522	−515	−490	−493	−479	−494	−488	−506	−6,000	−2,757	−10,724
Interior:													
Cancel Southern Nevada Public Land Management Act balances [3]		−83	−69	−78								−230	−230
Repeal enhanced geothermal payments to counties		−4	−4	−4	−4	−4	−4	−4	−4	−4	−4	−20	−40
Reauthorize the Federal Lands Recreation Enhancement Act		260	715	1,040	1,300	1,300	1,040	585	260			4,615	6,500
Establish a Public Lands Infrastructure Fund		173	642	958	1,296	1,296	1,036	581	256			4,365	6,230
Total, Interior													
Justice:													
Reform the Crime Victims Fund to preserve long-term solvency		−1,962	−1,623	−1,334	−868	3	85	105	45			−5,784	−5,549
Labor:													
Reform Pension Benefit Guaranty Corporation premiums		15	−4,109	−3,079	−2,749	2,208	−7,971	−2,810	−2,792	−2,825	−2,894	−7,714	−27,006
Expand Foreign Labor Certification fees													

Table S-6. Mandatory and Receipt Proposals—Continued

(Deficit increases (+) or decreases (−) in millions of dollars)

	2020	2021	2022	2023	2024	2025	2026	2027	2028	2029	2030	Totals 2021–2025	Totals 2021–2030
Reform the Federal Employees' Compensation Act		−31	−24	−28	−16	−17	−17	−19	−19	−21	−20	−116	−212
Reform the Trade Adjustment Assistance program		−55	−119	−133	6	55	23	−2	−28	−50	−75	−246	−378
Increase H–1B filing fee to fund training and education		−328	−211	−112	−18							−669	−669
Provide paid parental leave benefits [3,7,8]		750	750	1,338	1,999	2,209	2,408	2,599	2,773	2,936	3,083	7,046	20,845
Improve Unemployment Insurance program solvency and program integrity [3,8]		−111	−234	−805	−1,213	−1,730	−1,092	−1,268	−1,452	−1,797	−376	−4,093	−10,078
Total, Labor		240	−3,947	−2,819	−1,991	2,725	−6,649	−1,500	−1,518	−1,757	−282	−5,792	−17,498
Transportation:													
Reauthorize surface transportation programs		945	2,676	4,078	5,342	6,651	8,052	9,513	11,076	12,708	14,403	19,692	75,444
Treasury:													
Increase and extend guarantee fee charged by Government-sponsored enterprises		−202	−1,053	−2,250	−3,588	−4,644	−5,291	−5,123	−4,587	−4,075	−3,625	−11,737	−34,438
Subject Financial Research Fund to appropriations [3,8]			41	−11	−18	−18	−18	−18	−18	−18	−18	−6	−96
Increase debt collection [3,9]		−86	−80	−80	−80	−80	−80	−80	−80	−81	−81	−406	−808
Improve tax administration, including program integrity [3]		−964	−1,359	−3,634	−5,399	−7,303	−9,550	−11,922	−12,956	−13,870	−14,643	−18,659	−81,600
Repeal specific energy-related tax credits [3]	36	−1,165	−1,229	−1,645	−1,798	−1,998	−2,046	−1,948	−1,739	−1,525	−1,370	−7,835	−16,463
Total, Treasury	36	−2,417	−3,680	−7,620	−10,883	−14,043	−16,985	−19,091	−19,380	−19,569	−19,737	−38,643	−133,405
Veterans Affairs (VA):													
Enhance burial benefits for veterans		2	2	6	2	3	3	11	2	5	6	15	42
Reinstate Cost of Living Adjustment round-down		−41	−78	−128	−188	−256	−282	−292	−316	−326	−345	−691	−2,252
Standardize and enhance VA Compensation and Pension benefit programs		−752	−840	−930	−1,022	−1,116	−1,212	−1,310	−1,409	−1,665	−1,425	−4,660	−11,681
Standardize and improve veteran vocational rehabilitation and education benefit programs		108	91	77	65	56	47	40	35	14	11	397	544
Standardize and improve Specially Adapted Housing programs													
Total, Veterans Affairs		−683	−825	−975	−1,143	−1,313	−1,444	−1,551	−1,688	−1,972	−1,753	−4,939	−13,347
Corps of Engineers:													
Divest Washington Aqueduct				−118								−118	−118
Reform inland waterways financing [3]		−180	−180	−180	−180	−180	−180	−180	−180	−180	−180	−900	−1,800
Total, Corps of Engineers		−180	−180	−298	−180	−180	−180	−180	−180	−180	−180	−1,018	−1,918
Environmental Protection Agency:													
Expand use of pesticide licensing fees		5	4	4	4	4	3	2	1	1	1	21	29
General Services Administration (GSA, including Federal retirement):													
Reform Federal retirement [3]		−2,087	−1,455	−4,272	−6,830	−8,775	−10,400	−11,593	−12,571	−13,569	−14,683	−23,419	−86,235
Reform administrative financing of Earned Benefits Trust Fund													
Modify the Federal Employees Health Benefits Program		1	1	1	1	1	1	1	1	1	1	5	10
Expand authority for GSA Disposal Fund				−224	−351	−371	−394	−417	−441	−467	−494	−946	−3,159
Establish a Federal Capital Revolving Fund		274	2,039	2,167	2,000	1,833	267	200	133	67		8,313	8,980
Total, General Services Administration (including Federal retirement)		−1,812	585	−2,328	−5,180	−7,312	−10,526	−11,809	−12,878	−13,968	−15,176	−16,047	−80,404

Table S–6. Mandatory and Receipt Proposals—Continued

(Deficit increases (+) or decreases (−) in millions of dollars)

	2020	2021	2022	2023	2024	2025	2026	2027	2028	2029	2030	Totals 2021–2025	Totals 2021–2030
Other Defense - Civil Programs:													
Consolidate authorities to order Reserve component members to perform duty	......	......	16	34	52	71	90	111	132	156	180	173	842
Other independent agencies:													
Postal Service:													
Reform the Postal Service	−2,209	−7,007	−7,481	−7,801	−8,261	−8,760	−9,275	−9,892	−10,535	−11,208	−11,200	−39,310	−91,420
Other		−222	−6,123	−1,221	−1,400	−1,470	−1,489	−1,509	−1,746	−1,771	−2,826	−10,436	−19,777
Total, other independent agencies	−2,209	−7,229	−13,604	−9,022	−9,661	−10,230	−10,764	−11,401	−12,281	−12,979	−14,026	−49,746	−111,197
Crosscutting reforms:													
Authorize additional Afghan Special Immigrant Visas		34	55	57	54	49	48	44	40	40	41	249	462
Eliminate allocations to the Housing Trust Fund and Capital Magnet Fund [3]		81	−352	−171	−219	−296	−359	−377	−390	−396	−402	−957	−2,881
Extend Joint Committee mandatory sequestration										10,518	−27,230	......	−16,712
Lease Shared Secondary Licenses		−50	−55	−55	−60	−65	−70	−70	−80	−80	−85	−285	−670
Improve clarity in worker classification and information reporting requirements [3]		29	37	10	−3	−8	−6	−4	−8	−10	−28	65	9
Improving payment accuracy Government-wide		−253	−295	−337	−379	−422	−443	−464	−506	−527	−590	−1,686	−4,216
Advance the President's health reform vision:													
President's health reform vision allowance [10]			−14,000	−42,000	−68,000	−98,000	−106,000	−113,000	−126,000	−135,000	−142,000	−222,000	−844,000
Repeal health taxes (non-add), advance President's health reform vision (non-add)	*1,385*	*8,431*	*12,380*	*8,610*	*28,867*	*22,243*	*25,749*	*29,173*	*21,371*	*36,649*	*53,567*	*80,530*	*247,039*
Subtotal, advance President's health reform vision (non-add)	*1,385*	*8,431*	*−1,620*	*−33,390*	*−39,133*	*−75,757*	*−80,251*	*−83,827*	*−104,629*	*−98,351*	*−88,433*	*−141,470*	*−596,961*
Reform welfare programs:													
Reform the Supplemental Nutrition Assistance Program		−15,348	−16,108	−17,413	−17,599	−18,013	−18,771	−18,887	−19,311	−20,127	−20,282	−84,481	−181,859
Reduce TANF block grant		−1,095	−1,442	−1,513	−1,547	−1,607	−1,603	−1,595	−1,615	−1,618	−1,594	−7,204	−15,229
Strengthen TANF		−608	−608	−608	−608	−608	−608	−608	−608	−608	−608	−3,040	−6,080
Eliminate the TANF Contingency Fund		9	11	13	14	17	20	22	24	26	28	64	184
Get noncustodial parents to work													
Strengthen Child Support enforcement and establishment		−14	−25	−39	−44	−50	−51	−53	−54	−56	−57	−172	−443
Discontinue SSBG funding to States and Territories		−1,360	−1,632	−1,700	−1,700	−1,700	−1,700	−1,700	−1,700	−1,700	−1,700	−8,092	−16,592
Shift SSBG expenditures to Foster Care and Permanency		18	23	24	24	25	25	25	25	25	25	114	239
Require social security number for Child Tax Credit, Earned Income Tax Credit, and credit for other dependents [3]		−1,927	−7,134	−7,250	−7,330	−7,488	−7,776	−8,027	−8,294	−8,631	−8,938	−31,129	−72,795
Promote Opportunity and Economic Mobility Demonstrations		22	41	60	79	98	78	59	40	21	2	300	500
Total, reform welfare programs		−20,303	−26,874	−28,426	−28,711	−29,326	−30,386	−30,764	−31,493	−32,668	−33,124	−133,640	−292,075
Reform Federal disability programs and improve payment integrity:													
Promote greater labor force participation [3]		96	74	2	162	301	−2,030	−4,452	−8,398	−12,105	−16,811	635	−43,161
Reform Federal disability programs [3]		−1,044	−1,434	−1,709	−1,891	−2,069	−2,184	−2,280	−2,433	−2,393	−2,552	−8,147	−19,989

Table S–6. Mandatory and Receipt Proposals—Continued

(Deficit increases (+) or decreases (−) in millions of dollars)

	2020	2021	2022	2023	2024	2025	2026	2027	2028	2029	2030	Totals 2021–2025	Totals 2021–2030
Improve Social Security Administration payment integrity	....	1	−406	−129	−671	−1,410	−2,021	−2,100	−2,047	−1,957	−1,812	−2,615	−12,552
Total, reform Federal disability programs and improve payment integrity	....	−947	−1,766	−1,836	−2,400	−3,178	−6,235	−8,832	−12,878	−16,455	−21,175	−10,127	−75,702
Support major investment in infrastructure	....	4,750	23,749	37,998	47,498	37,998	18,999	9,500	4,749	4,749	....	151,993	189,990
Total, crosscutting reforms		−16,659	−19,501	−34,760	−52,220	−93,248	−124,452	−143,967	−166,566	−169,829	−224,593	−216,388	−1,045,795
Total, Mandatory Initiatives and Savings	**−1,425**	**−46,156**	**−88,623**	**−117,784**	**−157,404**	**−209,387**	**−276,161**	**−302,674**	**−337,901**	**−349,803**	**−417,704**	**−619,354**	**−2,303,597**

Note:

A more detailed version of this table, including breakouts of other lines, is available at https://whitehouse.gov/omb/budget/.

For receipt effects, positive figures indicate lower receipts. For outlay effects, positive figures indicate higher outlays. For net costs, positive figures indicate higher deficits.

[1] The single income-driven repayment plan proposal has interactive effects with the other student loan proposals. These effects are included in the single income-driven repayment plan subtotal.

[2] Savings are less than $500,000 in each year.

[3] The estimates for this proposal include effects on receipts. The receipt effects are detailed in the extended table online (https://whitehouse.gov/omb/budget/).

[4] Estimates were not available at the time of Budget publication.

[5] Reflects net savings to the Government. The proposal is estimated to save Medicare $215.4 billion (2021–2030) and save Medicaid $22.4 billion (2021–2030). The proposal increases spending from the General Fund by $185.7 billion (2021–2030).

[6] Reflects net savings to the Government. The proposal would reduce Medicare spending by $174.2 billion (2021–2030), while increasing spending from the General Fund by $86.3 billion (2021–2030).

[7] The paid parental leave proposal consists of $28.1 billion in benefit and program administration costs, offset by $7.3 billion in savings associated with increased State revenues.

[8] Net of income offsets.

[9] This proposal is revenue neutral for Federal scoring purposes. Estimated recoveries of $140.8 million for State taxes over the 10-year budget window.

[10] These amounts were enacted in Public Law 116–94 and are reflected in the baseline accordingly.

Table S–7. Proposed Discretionary Funding Levels in 2021 Budget

(Net budget authority in billions of dollars)

	2020	2021	2022	2023	2024	2025	2026	2027	2028	2029	2030	Totals, 2021-2030
Defense:												
Current Law Funding Levels[1]	667	672	688	705	722	740	758	776	796	815	836	7,506
Proposed Base Changes[2]	......	......	+51	+50	+59	+58	+40	+22	+2	–17	–38	+228
Defense Cap Adjustments:[3]												
Emergency Requirements	8	......	......	20	10	10	10	10	10	10	10	179
Overseas Contingency Operations	72	69	20	......	......	......	......	......	......	......	......	......
Total, Defense	746	741	759	775	791	808	808	808	808	808	808	7,914
Non-Defense:												
Current Law Funding Levels[1]	622	627	642	657	674	690	707	724	742	761	780	7,003
Proposed Base Changes[2]	......	–37	–64	–90	–119	–146	–174	–201	–230	–259	–288	–1,607
Proposed Base Funding	622	590	578	567	555	544	533	523	512	502	492	5,396
Federal Employee Retirement Cost Share Reduction Proposal.[4]	......	......	–6	–7	–9	–10	–10	–10	–10	–10	–10	–82
Non-Defense Cap Adjustments:												
Overseas Contingency Operations[5]	8	......	......	......	......	......	......	......	......	......	......	......
Emergency Requirements	1	......	......	......	......	......	......	......	......	......	......	......
Program Integrity	2	2	3	4	4	5	5	5	5	5	5	44
Disaster Relief	18	5	5	5	5	5	5	5	5	5	5	51
Wildfire Suppression	2	2	2	2	2	2	2	2	2	2	2	24
2020 Census	3	......	......	......	......	......	......	......	......	......	......	......
Total, Non-Defense Cap Adjustments	33	10	10	11	12	12	12	13	13	13	13	118
Total, Non-Defense with all Adjustments	655	600	582	571	558	547	535	525	514	505	495	5,432
Total, Discretionary Budget Authority	1,401	1,340	1,341	1,346	1,349	1,355	1,343	1,333	1,322	1,313	1,303	13,346
Memorandum - Appropriations Counted Outside of Discretionary Caps:												
21st Century Cures Appropriations[6]	1	*	1	1	1	*	*	......	......	......	......	3
Non-BBEDCA Emergency Funding[7]	–*	–5	......	......	......	......	......	......	......	......	......	–5

* $500 million or less.

[1] The current law funding levels presented here are equal to the caps for 2020 and 2021 in the Balanced Budget and Emergency Deficit Control Act of 1985 (BBEDCA) for "defense" (or Function 050) and "non-defense" (NDD) programs. For 2022 through 2030, programs are assumed to grow at current services growth rates.

[2] The 2021 Budget proposes to fund base defense programs for 2021 at the existing BBEDCA cap and fund base NDD programs at a level that is five percent below the 2020 NDD cap. After 2021, when the current caps expire, the Administration proposes to extend the BBEDCA caps through 2025 at the levels included in the 2021 Budget. This would provide an increase in defense funding of about two percent each year, and decrease funding for NDD programs by two percent (or "2-penny") each year. After 2025, the 2021 Budget sets placeholder levels that project current policies with defense programs frozen at the 2025 level while NDD programs continue the 2-penny reduction through the budget window.

Table S–7. Proposed Discretionary Funding Levels in 2021 Budget—Continued

(Net budget authority in billions of dollars)

[3] The 2021 Budget includes Overseas Contingency Operations (OCO) funding for defense programs in 2021 at the $69 billion level included in the Bipartisan Budget Act of 2019. After 2021, for the remaining years of the Future Years Defense Program (FYDP) and the Administration's proposed caps, OCO amounts would be $20 billion for 2022 and 2023 and $10 billion for 2024 and 2025, consistent with a potential transition of certain OCO costs into the base budget while continuing to fund contingency operations. After 2025, the 2021 Budget continues a notional $10 billion placeholder for OCO. Note that outyear OCO amounts do not reflect any specific decisions or assumptions about OCO funding in any particular year.

[4] This adjustment reflects savings from a reform proposed in the 2021 Budget that would reduce Federal agency costs through changes to current civilian employee retirement plans. After 2021, the Administration supports reductions to its proposed NDD caps and outyear levels for this reform.

[5] The 2021 Budget continues the Administration's policy to shift NDD OCO amounts into base discretionary funding. No NDD OCO amounts are proposed in 2021 or the outyears.

[6] The 21st Century Cures Act permitted funds to be appropriated each year and not counted towards the discretionary caps so long as the appropriations were specifically provided for the authorized purposes. These amounts are displayed outside of the discretionary totals for this reason and the levels included through the budget window reflect authorized levels.

[7] These are enacted rescissions or proposed permanent cancellations of balances of emergency funding that were not designated pursuant to BBEDCA. These amounts are not re-designated as emergency; therefore no savings are being achieved under the caps nor will the caps be adjusted for these amounts.

Table S–8.   2021 Discretionary Overview by Major Agency

(Net budget authority in billions of dollars)

	2019 Actual[1]	2020 Enacted[1]	2021 Request	2021 Request less 2020 Enacted	
				Dollar	Percent
Base Discretionary Funding:					
Cabinet Departments:					
Agriculture[2]	24.4	23.8	21.8	-1.9	-8.2%
Commerce[3]	11.6	12.9	8.1	-4.8	-37.3%
Defense	616.2	633.3	636.4	+3.1	+0.5%
Education	70.5	72.2	66.6	-5.6	-7.8%
Energy	35.6	38.5	35.4	-3.1	-8.1%
National Nuclear Security Administration	15.1	16.6	19.8	+3.2	+19.0%
Other Energy	20.5	21.9	15.6	-6.3	-28.7%
Health and Human Services (HHS)[4]	100.8	105.8	96.4	-9.5	-9.0%
Homeland Security (DHS)[5]	47.3	48.1	49.7	+1.6	+3.4%
Housing and Urban Development (HUD):					
HUD gross total (excluding receipts)	53.8	56.5	47.9	-8.6	-15.2%
HUD receipts	-9.5	-6.6	-8.8	-2.2	+33.8%
Interior	14.1	14.7	12.7	-2.0	-13.4%
Justice	30.8	32.4	31.7	-0.7	-2.3%
Labor	12.0	12.4	11.0	-1.3	-10.7%
State and Other International Programs (OIP)[2,6]	48.2	47.7	44.1	-3.7	-7.7%
State and OIP, including OCO funding (non-add)	56.2	55.7	44.1	-11.7	-20.9%
Transportation	26.5	24.8	21.6	-3.2	-12.9%
Treasury[5]	15.0	15.5	15.7	+0.2	+1.5%
Veterans Affairs	86.6	92.7	105.0	+12.3	+13.3%
Major Agencies:					
Corps of Engineers	7.0	7.7	6.0	-1.7	-22.0%
Environmental Protection Agency	8.9	9.1	6.7	-2.4	-26.5%
National Aeronautics and Space Administration	21.5	22.6	25.2	+2.7	+11.9%
National Science Foundation	8.1	8.3	7.7	-0.5	-6.5%
Small Business Administration (SBA)	0.7	0.8	0.7	-0.1	-11.1%
Social Security Administration (SSA)[4]	9.1	9.2	9.0	-0.2	-1.8%
Other Agencies	21.7	22.0	20.1	-1.9	-8.5%
Changes in mandatory programs[1]	-15.7	-15.9	-9.1	+6.8	-43.0%
Subtotal, Base Discretionary Funding	**1,244.8**	**1,288.2**	**1,261.5**	**-26.7**	**-2.1%**
Defense Base Subtotal	*647.0*	*666.5*	*671.5*	*+5.0*	*+0.8%*
Non-Defense Base Subtotal	*597.8*	*621.7*	*590.0*	*-31.7*	*-5.1%*

Table S–8. 2021 Discretionary Overview by Major Agency—Continued

(Net budget authority in billions of dollars)

	2019 Actual[1]	2020 Enacted[1]	2021 Request	2021 Request less 2020 Enacted	
				Dollar	Percent
Funding Above Base Discretionary Appropriations, including Cap Adjustments:					
Overseas Contingency Operations (OCO):					
Defense	68.8	71.3	69.0	–2.3	–3.2%
DHS	0.2	0.2	......	–0.2	–100.0%
State and Other International Programs	8.0	8.0	......	–8.0	–100.0%
Subtotal, OCO	77.0	79.5	69.0	–10.5	–13.2%
Emergency Requirements:					
Agriculture	5.1	......	......	......	......
Commerce	0.9	......	......	......	......
Defense	2.8	8.0	......	–8.0	–100.0%
HHS	3.2	0.5	......	–0.5	–100.0%
DHS	1.9	......	......	......	......
HUD	4.1	......	......	......	......
Interior	0.4	......	......	......	......
Justice	0.2	......	......	......	......
Transportation	1.7	......	......	......	......
Corps of Engineers	3.3	......	......	......	......
Environmental Protection Agency	0.4	......	......	......	......
Other Agencies	0.7	......	......	......	......
Allowance for USMCA Implementation[7]	......	0.8	......	–0.8	–100.0%
Subtotal, Emergency Requirements	24.3	9.4	......	–9.4	–100.0%
Program Integrity:					
HHS	0.5	0.5	0.5	+0.0	+4.4%
Labor	*	0.1	0.1	+0.0	+43.1%
Treasury[8]	......	......	0.4	+0.4	N/A
SSA	1.4	1.3	1.3	–*	–0.5%
Subtotal, Program Integrity	1.9	1.8	2.3	+0.4	+23.8%
Disaster Relief:					
DHS	12.0	17.4	5.1	–12.3	–70.8%
SBA	......	0.2	......	–0.2	–100.0%
Subtotal, Disaster Relief	12.0	17.5	5.1	–12.4	–71.1%
Wildfire Suppression:					
Agriculture	......	2.0	2.0	+0.1	+4.6%
Interior	......	0.3	0.3	+*	+3.3%
Subtotal, Wildfire Suppression	......	2.3	2.4	+0.1	+4.4%
2020 Census:					
Commerce	......	2.5	......	–2.5	–100.0%

Table S–8. 2021 Discretionary Overview by Major Agency—Continued

(Net budget authority in billions of dollars)

	2019 Actual[1]	2020 Enacted[1]	2021 Request	2021 Request less 2020 Enacted	
				Dollar	Percent
Non-BBEDCA Emergency Appropriations:					
HUD and Energy[9]	....	—*	-4.8	-4.8	N/A
21st Century Cures Appropriations:[10]					
HHS	0.8	0.6	0.5	-0.1	-16.4%
Subtotal, Above Base Funding, including Cap Adjustments	**116.0**	**113.5**	**74.3**	**-39.2**	**-34.5%**
Total, Discretionary Budget Authority	**1,360.8**	**1,401.7**	**1,335.8**	**-65.9**	**-4.7%**
Defense Total	*718.8*	*746.0*	*740.5*	*-5.5*	*-0.7%*
Non-Defense Total	*641.9*	*655.7*	*595.3*	*-60.4*	*-9.2%*

* $50 million or less.

1 The 2019 actual and 2020 enacted levels include changes that occur after appropriations are enacted that are part of budget execution such as transfers, reestimates, and the rebasing as mandatory any changes in mandatory programs (CHIMPs) enacted in appropriations bills. The 2019 and 2020 levels are adjusted to include OMB's scoring of CHIMPs enacted in 2019 and 2020 appropriations Acts for base programs for a better illustrative comparison with the 2021 request.

2 Funding for Food for Peace Title II Grants is included in the State and Other International Programs total. Although the funds are appropriated to the Department of Agriculture, the funds are administered by the U.S. Agency for International Development (USAID).

3 The large decrease in 2021 for the Department of Commerce is mostly attributable to the ramp down of the 2020 Decennial Census.

4 Funding from the Hospital Insurance and Supplementary Medical Insurance trust funds for administrative expenses incurred by SSA that support the Medicare program are included in the HHS total and not in the SSA total.

5 The funding totals for 2019 actual and 2020 enacted are comparatively adjusted to reflect the Administration's 2021 Budget proposal to shift the U.S. Secret Service from DHS to the Department of the Treasury.

6 The State and International Programs total includes funding for the Department of State, USAID, Treasury International, and 12 international agencies.

7 At the time the Budget was finalized, Public Law 116–113, the United States-Mexico-Canada (USMCA) Agreement Implementation Act had not been enacted. As a result, the Budget includes a Government-wide allowance to represent the discretionary appropriations included in this proposal.

8 The Budget proposes a new cap adjustment related to program integrity in the Internal Revenue Service. See the Budget Process chapter of the *Analytical Perspectives* volume of the Budget for more information on this adjustment.

9 The final 2020 appropriations Act rescinded remaining balances of emergency funding in HUD that were not designated pursuant to BBEDCA. These rescissions were not re-designated as emergency, therefore no savings were scored under the caps and the caps were not adjusted for these rescissions. The 2021 Budget proposes similar permanent cancellations of non-BBEDCA emergency funds to eliminate the Title 17 Innovative Technology Loan Guarantee Program and the Advanced Technology Vehicles Manufacturing Loan Program in the Department of Energy.

10 The 21st Century Cures Act permitted funds to be appropriated each year for certain activities and not counted toward the discretionary caps so long as the appropriations were specifically provided for the authorized purposes.

Table S–9. Economic Assumptions[1]
(Calendar years)

| | Actual | | Projections | | | | | | | | | | |
	2018	2019	2020	2021	2022	2023	2024	2025	2026	2027	2028	2029	2030
Gross Domestic Product (GDP):													
Nominal level, billions of dollars	20,580	21,437	22,494	23,645	24,849	26,113	27,442	28,822	30,242	31,719	33,269	34,893	36,598
Percent change, nominal GDP, year/year	5.4	4.2	4.9	5.1	5.1	5.1	5.1	5.0	4.9	4.9	4.9	4.9	4.9
Real GDP, percent change, year/year	2.9	2.4	2.8	3.1	3.0	3.0	3.0	3.0	2.9	2.8	2.8	2.8	2.8
Real GDP, percent change, Q4/Q4	2.5	2.5	3.1	3.0	3.0	3.0	3.0	2.9	2.8	2.8	2.8	2.8	2.8
GDP chained price index, percent change, year/year	2.4	1.8	2.0	2.0	2.0	2.0	2.0	2.0	2.0	2.0	2.0	2.0	2.0
Consumer Price Index,[2] percent change, year/year	2.4	1.8	2.2	2.3	2.3	2.3	2.3	2.3	2.3	2.3	2.3	2.3	2.3
Interest rates, percent:[3]													
91-day Treasury bills[4]	1.9	2.1	1.4	1.5	1.5	1.6	1.7	2.0	2.2	2.4	2.5	2.5	2.5
10-year Treasury notes	2.9	2.2	2.0	2.2	2.5	2.7	3.0	3.1	3.1	3.1	3.2	3.2	3.2
Unemployment rate, civilian, percent[3]	3.9	3.7	3.5	3.6	3.8	4.0	4.0	4.0	4.0	4.0	4.0	4.0	4.0

Note: A more detailed table of economic assumptions appears in Chapter 2, "Economic Assumptions and Interactions with the Budget," in the *Analytical Perspectives* volume of the Budget.

[1] Based on information available as of mid-November 2019.
[2] Seasonally adjusted CPI for all urban consumers.
[3] Annual average.
[4] Average rate, secondary market (bank discount basis).

Table S–10. Federal Government Financing and Debt

(Dollar amounts in billions)

	Actual 2019	Estimate 2020	2021	2022	2023	2024	2025	2026	2027	2028	2029	2030
Financing:												
Unified budget deficit:												
Primary deficit/surplus (−)	609	707	588	521	319	94	27	−62	−150	−146	−395	−404
Net interest	375	376	378	399	428	458	499	543	586	621	645	665
Unified budget deficit	984	1,083	966	920	746	552	527	481	435	475	250	261
As a percent of GDP	4.6%	4.9%	4.1%	3.7%	2.9%	2.0%	1.8%	1.6%	1.4%	1.4%	0.7%	0.7%
Other transactions affecting borrowing from the public:												
Changes in financial assets and liabilities:[1]												
Change in Treasury operating cash balance	−2	3	......	......	......	......	......	......	......	......	......	......
Net disbursements of credit financing accounts:												
Direct loan and Troubled Asset Relief Program (TARP) equity purchase accounts	43	−16	67	63	54	46	41	35	33	31	27	27
Guaranteed loan accounts	28	12	−1	−2	−2	−1	−1	−2	−3	−4	−*	1
Net purchases of non-Federal securities by the National Railroad Retirement Investment Trust (NRRIT)	−1	−1	−1	−1	−1	−1	−1	−1	−1	−1	−1	−*
Net change in other financial assets and liabilities[2]	*											
Subtotal, changes in financial assets and liabilities	68	−3	65	59	52	44	38	33	29	26	27	28
Seigniorage on coins	−1	−*	−*	−*	−*	−*	−*	−*	−*	−*	−*	−*
Total, other transactions affecting borrowing from the public	67	−3	65	59	51	43	38	32	29	26	26	27
Total, requirement to borrow from the public (equals change in debt held by the public)	1,051	1,080	1,031	979	798	595	565	514	464	501	276	289
Changes in Debt Subject to Statutory Limitation:												
Change in debt held by the public	1,051	1,080	1,031	979	798	595	565	514	464	501	276	289
Change in debt held by Government accounts	156	150	146	103	123	164	103	101	−1	−87	92	−46
Change in other factors	5	3	2	2	2	2	1	1	2	1	1	*
Total, change in debt subject to statutory limitation	1,212	1,233	1,179	1,084	922	761	668	615	465	415	369	242
Debt Subject to Statutory Limitation, End of Year:												
Debt issued by Treasury	22,647	23,878	25,056	26,138	27,059	27,820	28,488	29,103	29,567	29,982	30,351	30,593
Adjustment for discount, premium, and coverage[3]	40	42	43	44	45	46	46	47	47	48	49	49
Total, debt subject to statutory limitation[4]	22,687	23,920	25,099	26,182	27,105	27,866	28,534	29,150	29,615	30,030	30,399	30,642
Debt Outstanding, End of Year:												
Gross Federal debt:[5]												
Debt issued by Treasury	22,647	23,878	25,056	26,138	27,059	27,820	28,488	29,103	29,567	29,982	30,351	30,593
Debt issued by other agencies	23	22	21	21	20	19	18	18	17	16	16	16
Total, gross Federal debt	22,669	23,900	25,077	26,159	27,080	27,839	28,506	29,121	29,584	29,998	30,366	30,609
As a percent of GDP	106.9%	107.6%	107.4%	106.6%	105.0%	102.7%	100.1%	97.4%	94.4%	91.3%	88.1%	84.6%

Table S–10. Federal Government Financing and Debt—Continued

(Dollar amounts in billions)

	Actual 2019	Estimate										
		2020	2021	2022	2023	2024	2025	2026	2027	2028	2029	2030
Held by:												
Debt held by Government accounts	5,869	6,019	6,165	6,269	6,391	6,555	6,658	6,759	6,758	6,671	6,763	6,717
Debt held by the public[6]	16,801	17,881	18,912	19,891	20,688	21,284	21,848	22,362	22,826	23,327	23,604	23,892
As a percent of GDP	79.2%	80.5%	81.0%	81.0%	80.2%	78.5%	76.7%	74.8%	72.8%	71.0%	68.5%	66.1%
Debt Held by the Public Net of Financial Assets:												
Debt held by the public	16,801	17,881	18,912	19,891	20,688	21,284	21,848	22,362	22,826	23,327	23,604	23,892
Less financial assets net of liabilities:												
Treasury operating cash balance	382	385	385	385	385	385	385	385	385	385	385	385
Credit financing account balances:												
Direct loan and TARP equity purchase accounts	1,415	1,399	1,466	1,529	1,584	1,630	1,671	1,706	1,739	1,770	1,797	1,824
Guaranteed loan accounts	32	44	43	41	39	38	37	35	33	29	29	29
Government-sponsored enterprise preferred stock	112	112	112	112	112	112	112	112	112	112	112	112
Non-Federal securities held by NRRIT	24	23	22	20	19	18	17	16	15	15	14	14
Other assets net of liabilities	–60	–60	–60	–60	–60	–60	–60	–60	–60	–60	–60	–60
Total, financial assets net of liabilities	1,906	1,904	1,969	2,028	2,080	2,123	2,162	2,195	2,224	2,251	2,277	2,305
Debt held by the public net of financial assets	14,894	15,977	16,943	17,863	18,609	19,160	19,686	20,167	20,602	21,077	21,327	21,587
As a percent of GDP	70.2%	71.9%	72.6%	72.8%	72.2%	70.7%	69.1%	67.5%	65.7%	64.1%	61.9%	59.7%

* $500 million or less.

[1] A decrease in the Treasury operating cash balance (which is an asset) is a means of financing a deficit and therefore has a negative sign. An increase in checks outstanding (which is a liability) is also a means of financing a deficit and therefore also has a negative sign.

[2] Includes checks outstanding, accrued interest payable on Treasury debt, uninvested deposit fund balances, allocations of special drawing rights, and other liability accounts; and, as an offset, cash and monetary assets (other than the Treasury operating cash balance), other asset accounts, and profit on sale of gold.

[3] Consists mainly of debt issued by the Federal Financing Bank (which is not subject to limit), the unamortized discount (less premium) on public issues of Treasury notes and bonds (other than zero-coupon bonds), and the unrealized discount on Government account series securities.

[4] Legislation enacted August 2, 2019 (Public Law 116—37), temporarily suspends the debt limit through July 31, 2021.

[5] Treasury securities held by the public and zero-coupon bonds held by Government accounts are almost all measured at sales price plus amortized discount or less amortized premium. Agency debt securities are almost all measured at face value. Treasury securities in the Government account series are otherwise measured at face value less unrealized discount (if any).

[6] At the end of 2019, the Federal Reserve Banks held $2,113.3 billion of Federal securities and the rest of the public $14,687.4 billion. Debt held by the Federal Reserve Banks is not estimated for future years.

OMB CONTRIBUTORS TO THE 2021 BUDGET

The following personnel contributed to the preparation of this publication. Hundreds, perhaps thousands, of others throughout the Government also deserve credit for their valuable contributions.

A

Lindsay Abate
Andrew Abrams
Chandana L. Achanta
Laurie Adams
Shagufta Ahmed
P. Joseph Ahn
Steve Aitken
Lina Al Sudani
Joseph Albanese
Jason Alleman
Victoria Allred
Aaron Alton
Vishal Amin
Nicholas Andersen
Rachel Arguello
Judith Arnold
William L. Arritt
Anna R. Arroyo
Emily Schultz Askew
Lisa L. August
Kristin B. Aveille

B

Drew Bailey
Jessie W. Bailey
Ally P. Bain
Paul W. Baker
Steven Bakovic
Carol A. Bales
Caroline Ball
Pratik S. Banjade
Avital Bar-Shalom
Carl Barrick
Jody Barringer
Amy Batchelor
Sarah Belford
Jennifer Wagner Bell
Anna M. Bellantoni
Sara Bencic
Sarah M. Bender
Nathaniel H.
    Benjamin

Joseph J. Berger
Elizabeth A. Bernhard
William Bestani
Madison Biedermann
Mark Bigley
Samuel J. Black
Catherine Bloniarz
Mathew C. Blum
Sharon A. Boivin
Amira C. Boland
Cassie L. Boles
Melissa B. Bomberger
David Bottom
William J. Boyd
James Braid
Michael Branson
Alex M. Brant
Joseph F. Breighner
Andrea M. Brian
Candice M. Bronack
Katherine W. Broomell
Dustin S. Brown
Sheila Bruce
Michael T. Brunetto
Grace Bruno
Pearl Buenvenida
Tom D. Bullers
Scott H. Burgess
Ben Burnett
Jordan C. Burris
John C. Burton
Nicholas S. Burton
Justin Buschow
Mark Bussow
Dylan W. Byrd

C

Steven Cahill
Ariella Campana
Amy Canfield
Eric D. Cardoza
Kevin Carpenter
Curtis M. Carr Jr.

Christina S. Carrere
Matthew T. Carroll
William S. S. Carroll
Scott D. Carson
Mary I. Cassell
David E. Cerrato
Taylor Chaffetz
James Chase
Nida Chaudhary
Maria Cheeks
Erin Cheese
Anita Chellaraj
Michael Clark
Angela Colamaria
Victoria W. Collin
Debra M. Collins
Kelly T. Colyar
Ann Conant
Jose A. Conde
Alyson M. Conley
David Connolly
Jeannette Mandycz
    Connor
Kyle Connors
Mary Rose Conroy
Shila Cooch
Aaron Cooke
LaTiesha B. Cooper
Matthew T. Cornelius
Patrick Corrigan
Drew W. Cramer
Catherine E. Crato
William Creedon
Rose Crow
Jefferson Crowder
James Crowe
Julie Crump
Craig Crutchfield
Justin Cruz
David M. Cruz-
    Glaudemans
Lily Cuk
Pennee Cumberlander
Laura Cunliffe

C. Tyler Curtis
William Curtis
Matthew Cutts

D

Gregory D'Angelo
D. Michael Daly
Rody Damis
Neil B. Danberg
Elisabeth C. Daniel
Kristy L. Daphnis
Alexander J. Daumit
Joanne Chow
    Davenport
Kenneth L. Davis
Margaret B. Davis-
    Christian
Tasha M. Demps
Paul J. Denaro
Laura Dennehy
Wesley Denton
Catherine A. Derbes
Antonio Diaz-Agosto
John H. Dick
Amie Didlo
Jean Diomi Kazadi
Angela M. Donatelli
Jessica Donlon
Paul S. Donohue
Vladik Dorjets
Michelle Dorsey
Tobias A. Dorsey
Anjelica B. Dortch
Megan Dreher
Lisa Cash Driskill
Julie Driver
Mark A. Dronfield
Michael P. Duffey
Vanessa Duguay

E

Matthew C. Eanes

Jacqueline A. Easley
Calie Edmonds
Jeanette Edwards
Michelle Enger
Diana F. Epstein
Brede Eschliman
Gillian Evans
Patrick Evans
Troy L. Ezell

F

Farnoosh Faezi-Marian
Robert Fairweather
Edna Falk Curtin
Hunter Fang
Kara L. Farley-Cahill
Christine E.
   Farquharson
Louis Feagans
Christopher M. Felix
Lesley A. Field
Michael Fierro
Hugh Fike
Leah R. Fine
Jonathan K. Finer
Sean C. Finnegan
Mary Fischietto
Brette Fishman
John J. Fitzpatrick
Mitchell L. Forbes
Daniel G. Fowlkes
Lindsay Fraser
Nicholas A. Fraser
Ashlea Frazier
Haley Friedman
Laurel Fuller

G

Abigail P. Gage
Scott D. Gaines
Christopher D.
   Gamache
Mar Gamboa
Joseph Gammello
Joseph R. Ganahl
Kyle Gardiner
Alexandria N. Gardner
Mathias A. Gardner
Marc Garufi
Anthony R. Garza
Mariam Ghavalyan
Daniel Giamo

Brian Gillis
Vance Ginn
Jacob Glass
Joshua S. Glazer
Andrea L. Goel
Jeffrey D. Goldstein
Lauren Gomez
Anthony A. Gonzalez
Oscar Gonzalez
Taylor J. Good
Alex Goodenough
Harrison D. Grafos
Michael Graham
Margie Graves
Aron Greenberg
Brandon H. Greene
Robin J. Griffin
Justin Grimes
Hester C. Grippando
Stephanie Grosser
Andrea L. Grossman
Kerry Gutknecht

H

Michael B. Hagan
Tia Hall
William F. Hamele
Amy Hamilton
Christine E. Hammer
Brian Hanson
Jennifer L. Hanson
David T. Hardin
Dionne Hardy
Deidre A. Harrison
Edward Hartwig
Paul Harvey
Laurel Havas
Nichole M. Hayden
Bradley Hayes
Mark Hazelgren
Edie M. Heipel
Peter Hendrickson
Elizabeth Hennemuth
John David Henson
Juan Manuel Heredia
Kevin W. Herms
Rachel Hernández
Alex Hettinger
Michael J. Hickey
Michael Hildner
Amanda M. Hill
Jonathan Hill
Elke Hodson-Marten

Jennifer E. Hoef
Jason Hoffman
Stuart Hoffman
Troy Holland
Brandon T. Holt
Michele Holt
Clinton T. Hourigan
Peter Hoy
Grace Hu
Rhea A. Hubbard
Kathy M. Hudgins
Shristi Humagai
Sally J. Hunnicutt
Alexander T. Hunt
Lorraine D. Hunt
William Hunt
James C. Hurban
Veta Hurst
Nathan Hurwitz

I

Tae H. Im
Davis Ingle

J

Theodore R. Jackson
Manish Jain
Harrison M. Jarrett
Carol Jenkins
Chase Jennings
Connor Jennings
Carol Johnson
Michael D. Johnson
Miles Johnson
Danielle Y. Jones
Denise Bray Jones
Lauren H. Jones
Lisa M. Jones
Othni A. Jones
Colby Ryan Jordan
Hee Jun

K

Derek Kan
Daniel S. Kaneshiro
Jacob H. Kaplan
Regina L. Kearney
Michelle Kelley
Nancy B. Kenly
Moses I. Kennedy
Suzette Kent

Meshach E. Keye
Shubha Khot
Jeongsoo Kim
Jung H. Kim
Maria Kim
Rachael Y. Kim
Kelly C. King
Kelly A. Kinneen
Jessica Kirby
Robert T. Klein
Kenneth A. Klukowski
Nick Koo
Andrea G. Korovesis
Katelyn V. Koschewa
Summer Kostelnik
Faride Kraft
Lori A. Krauss
Steven B. Kuennen
Robert Kuhlman
Jennifer J. Kuk
Christine Kymn

L

Christopher D. LaBaw
Jonathan W. Ladyga
Leonard L. Lainhart
Chad A. Lallemand
Lawrence L. Lambert
Adrienne-Elaine
   Lamptey
Michael Landry
Daniel LaPlaca
Anthony Larkins
Ashley P. Lau
Eric P. Lauer
Jessie L. LaVine
Christopher Leach
Jessica Lee
Susan E. Leetmaa
Bryan León
Kerrie Leslie
John Levock-Spindle
James A. Lewis
Sheila Lewis
Wendy L. Liberante
Richard Alan
   Lichtenberger
Andrew Lieberman
Jennifer Liebschutz
Kristina E. Lilac
Erika Liliedahl
John E. Lindner
Adam Lipton

Kim Lopez
Sara R. Lopez
Adrienne Lucas
Gideon F. Lukens

M

Deborah Macaulay
Ryan MacMaster
Claire A. Mahoney
Dominic J. Mancini
Noah S. Mann
Roman Manziyenko
Sharon Mar
Michelle Marston
Italy Martin
Rochelle Martinez
Kimie Matsuo
Salim Mawani
Jessica Rae McBean
Alexander J.
  McClelland
Malcolm McConnell
Brian McCormack
Jeremy P. McCrary
Anthony W. McDonald
Christine A. McDonald
Katrina A. McDonald
Renford McDonald
Natalie McIntyre
Charlie E. McKiver
Michael McManus
William McNavage
Christopher McNeal
Barbara A. Menard
Flavio Menasce
Margaret Mergen
P. Thaddeus
  Messenger
William L. Metzger
Lauren Michaels
Daniel J. Michelson-
  Horowitz
Julie L. Miller
Kimberly Miller
Sofie Miller
Susan M. Minson
Emily A. Mok
Kirsten J. Moncada
Claire Monteiro
Joseph Montoni
Julia C. Moore
Hallee Morgan
William Morrison

Robin McLaughry
  Mullins
Mick Mulvaney
Jonathan Murphy
Christian G. Music
Hayley W. Myers
Kimberley L Myers

N

Jeptha E. Nafziger
Larry J. Nagl
Barry Napear
Robert Nassif
Kimberly P. Nelson
Melissa K. Neuman
Caitlyn Newhard
Joanie F. Newhart
Christine Nguy
Teresa O. Nguyen
Tim H. Nusraty
Joseph B. Nye

O

Erin O'Brien
Kerry Clinton O'Dell
Matthew J. O'Kane
Brendan J. O'Meara
Melanie Ofiesh
Matthew Oreska
Denis A. Ortega
Jared Ostermiller
Michon Oubichon

P

Heather C. Pajak
Rosario Palmieri
Mark R. Paoletta
Peggy A. Parker
John C. Pasquantino
Neal A. Patel
Brian Paxton
Casey Pearce
Liuyi Pei
Falisa L. Peoples-Tittle
Michael A. Perz
Whitney L. Peters
William C. Petersen
Andrea M. Petro
Amy E. Petz
Stacey Que-Chi Pham
Carolyn R. Phelps

Karen A. Pica
Brian Pickeral
Brian Pipa
Joseph Pipan
Jeffrey S. Pollack
Mark J. Pomponio
Ruxandra Pond
Julianne Poston
Nancy Potok
Larrimer S. Prestosa
Jamie M. Price
Alanna B. Pugliese
Robert B. Purdy

R

Lucas R. Radzinschi
Latonda Glass Raft
Joseph Ramallo
Houman Rasouli
Johnnie Ray
Alex Reed
Paul B. Rehmus
Thomas M. Reilly
Bryant D. Renaud
Taylor N. Riccard
Keri A. Rice
Natalie Rico
Kyle S. Riggs
Jamal Rittenberry
Beth Higa Roberts
Taylor C. Roberts
Donovan Robinson
Wandlyn Robinson
Claudia G. Roche
Marshall J. Rodgers
Christina M.
  Rodriguez
Samantha Romero
Meredith B. Romley
Stephanie D. Rosch
Jeffrey R. Ross
Sean Rough
David J. Rowe
Amanda Roy
Danielle Royal
Tamia Russell
Erika H. Ryan

S

Adam N. Salazar
John Asa Saldivar
Mark S. Sandy

Nathan T. Sanfilippo
Ruth Saunders
Gregoire F. Sauter
Joel Savary
Jason Sawyer
Grant Schneider
Ansley Schoen
Daniel K. Schory
Nancy E. Schwartz
Mariarosaria
  Sciannameo
Jasmeet K. Seehra
Kimberly Segura
Robert B. Seidner
Andrew Self
Rachel Semmel
Megan Shade
Shahid N. Shah
Shabnam
  Sharbatoghlie
Amy K. Sharp
Dianne Shaughnessy
Paul Shawcross
David Shorkrai
Gary F. Shortencarrier
Leticia Sierra
Sara R. Sills
Celeste Simon
Daniel Liam Singer
Sarah Sisaye
Robert Sivinski
Benjamin J. Skidmore
Richard A. Skokowski
Curtina O. Smith
Sarah B. Smith
Stannis M. Smith
Silvana Solano
Roderic A. Solomon
Timothy F. Soltis
Amanda R.K. Sousane
Rebecca L. Spavins
Valeria Spinner
John H. Spittell
Sarah Whittle Spooner
Travis C. Stalcup
Scott R. Stambaugh
Nora Stein
David Stepp
Lamar R. Stewart
Ryan Stoffers
Gary R. Stofko
Terry W. Stratton
Thomas J. Suarez
Kevin J. Sullivan

Jessica L. Sun
Katherine M. Sydor

T

Jamie R. Taber
Naomi S. Taransky
Emma K. Tessier
Satya Thallam
Rich Theroux
Amanda L. Thomas
Payton A. Thomas
Will Thomas
Parth Tikiwala
Thomas Tobasko
Gia Tonic
Gil M. Tran
Katherine Trout
Susanna Troxler
Austin Turner

U

Nicholas J. Ufier
Shraddha A.
   Upadhyaya
Darrell J. Upshaw
Taylor J. Urbanski

V

Matthew J. Vaeth
Areletha L. Venson
Alexandra Ventura
Cesar Villanueva
Russ Vought
Megha Vyas

W

Dana Wade
James A. Wade
Brett Waite
Nicole Waldeck

Traci Walker
Heather V. Walsh
Tim Wang
Peter Warren
Gary Waxman
Bess M. Weaver
Jacqueline K. Webb
Margaret Weichert
Jeffrey A. Weinberg
David Weisshaar
Philip R. Wenger
Max West
Arnette C. White
Ashley M. White
Curtis C. White
Kim S. White
Sherron R. White
Brian Widuch
Rayna Wilkins
Debbie L. Williams
Rebecca Williams
Jamie S. Wilson
Paul A. Winters

James Wolff
Minzy Won
Raymond J.M. Wong
Jacob Wood
Bryn Woollacott
Michael Wooten
Sophia M. Wright
Bert Wyman

Y

Jason Yaworske
Melany N. Yeung
David Y. Yi
Christian T. Yonkeu
Rita Young
Janice Yun

Z

Eliana M. Zavala